FOUR LECTURES ON SHAKESPEARE

ELLEN TERRY

FOUR LECTURES ON
SHAKESPEARE

Edited with an Introduction by
CHRISTOPHER ST. JOHN

MARTIN HOPKINSON LTD
23 SOHO SQUARE LONDON

FIRST PUBLISHED APRIL 1932

CONTENTS

INTRODUCTION

ELLEN TERRY gave these Shakespearean lectures, or discourses as she preferred to call them, at various times in various places in Great Britain, America, Australia and New Zealand for a period of about ten years (1911 to 1921). With the exception of 'The Letters in Shakespeare's Plays', which appeared in *The Atlantic Monthly* in America, and in *The Windsor Magazine* in England, in December 1921, the lectures have not been published in any form until now. Negotiations for their publication were frequently started in Ellen Terry's lifetime, but came to nothing for many reasons, only two of which need be given here. Naturally editors and publishers were most keenly interested in the lectures at the time Ellen Terry was delivering them, but she was then opposed to their being made accessible in print, chiefly on the ground that they had been composed to be heard, not to be read. She appealed to me as her literary henchman for advice, and I agreed that without the improvisations she made when she was lecturing, without the illumination of her views and

7

ideas provided by her acting of the interpolated scenes, her lectures would be only half themselves. Readers who had not heard them might wonder why scholarly critics had welcomed them as an important contribution to the study of Shakespeare, and why they had proved immensely popular with the general public. When Ellen Terry's apparently inexhaustible store of youth and vigour, which enabled her to keep old age at bay until she had entered her seventy-sixth year, gave out, and she was forced to retire from public life, I recalled the proverb that half a loaf is better than no bread, and urged her to prepare a version of her lectures for publication. But by that time she was tragically unequal to the task.

I have spoken of myself as her 'literary henchman', and it is true that from the year 1903, the date at which my friendship with her daughter Edith Craig established a close relationship with her, she invoked my services on all occasions when she had to write something for publication, or make a speech, or give an interview. I am the more willing to admit this, now that the publication of some of her best letters, those written to Bernard Shaw, has proved conclusively that a collaborator was a convenience to her rather than a necessity. She had no difficulty whatever in expressing herself in writing. Her literary style, graceful,

vivid and direct, might make many skilled professional authors green with envy. Bernard Shaw remarked, when he brought Edith Craig his collection of
letters from Ellen Terry, with the suggestion that they
should be published separately : ' She had naturally
that simplicity of expression which it takes most writers
years of hard labour to acquire.' I know that I learned
more about the art of writing from her than from
anyone else. I often felt at the time I was assisting her
in the composition of her autobiography that I was
the apprentice and she the master craftsman.

' Oh, I couldn't say that ! ' she would exclaim as I
read her my written record of some incident in her life
she had related to me. ' Well, how would you like it
put ? ' I would ask, rather mortified, for I had taken
great pains to put off myself, and put on Ellen Terry,
in the passage she had interrupted. Immediately, if she
were in the mood, she would flash out ' how ' in living
phrases which made my own more ' literary' ones seem
dull, pompous, stiff stuff in which not a breath of life
stirred. My value to her as a collaborator did not
consist so much in the skill with the pen I had acquired
in the practice of my profession, as in my ability to
control my self-esteem when it threatened to become
troublesome and be an obstacle to my surrender to her
wishes.

The system on which we worked at these lectures was much the same as that we had adopted in her autobiography, published in 1907 under the title *The Story of My Life*. Ellen Terry, by her side a Globe edition of Shakespeare, on the title-page of which she had written ' Sir, here is a poor friend of yours that loves you', talked, and I made notes. Sometimes I became so much absorbed in watching ' the lovely nervous knitting of Ellen Terry's brows ' (Rebecca West's fine phrase) that I wrote without looking at the paper, and this blind writing was often illegible. Perhaps we ought to have had an efficient shorthand-writer in the room during those debates, in which I often played the part of the devil's advocate, disputing Ellen Terry's theories as the best method of inducing her to tell me how she had arrived at them, but it would have been difficult to arrange, as they took place at odd hours in odd places, and were frequently interrupted.

From the rough scenario supplied by my notes, I would labour to construct something answering to the description of a lecture. At different stages of its progress I used to show it to Edith Craig, a discriminating critic, and her helpful ' That's not a bit like mother ' led to the excision of a great many stilted literary expressions. The thing was more ' like mother ' by the time it was in a state to be read to her. The day she snatched the manuscript away from me, the want of variety in the pace of my reading having made her impatient, and began reading it to me with impromptu additions, I was satisfied that out of this material, quarried originally from her mind, and then rough-hewn by me, she would be able to create something in her own image.

This creation occupied her for a long time. When she first delivered the lecture, several copies of which she had printed in a type large and bold enough for her to read it without spectacles, she adhered more or less faithfully to the original version. By 1915 she had transformed it with cuts, transpositions, and the incorporation of many of her platform improvisations. The critic of *The Times* who wrote after hearing her lecture on the pathetic heroines of Shakespeare that ' wherever and whenever she speaks it will always be different and always fresh ' may not have meant that she would never give the same lecture, but this is what actually happened. Not only did she make several different versions for different types of audiences ; she gave each particular audience improvisations inspired by its response. The text printed here is a blend of the four texts she used most frequently during her tours.

The idea of her lecturing originated as far back as the year 1903 when she was touring the provinces with her own company in a repertory of plays. She consented during her visit to Glasgow to give a talk on Shakespeare in aid of the funds of the local branch of The Ladies' Theatrical Guild. She considered several subjects for this talk, among them 'Shakespeare's Children', but eventually chose 'The Letters in Shakespeare's Plays', chiefly because she was under the impression that they had never been talked or written about before.[1] She was very jubilant at having discovered what she described as 'a neglected corner of Shakespeare's world', and had a special affection for this lecture, first given at Glasgow to a very small audience. She included it in her repertory, when she went to the United States in 1910 to give a series of lectures, but it never went as well with audiences as its successors. The lectures on Shakespeare's Heroines were the most popular. They gave Ellen Terry better opportunities for exercising her own art and in time became an epitome of her Shakespearean impersonations. Some idea of the impression they made when first given in London at the Haymarket Theatre in May 1911 can be gathered from the following pas-

---

[1] The only book I know on the subject, *Shakespeare as a Letter-Writer*, by R. L. Mégroz, was not published until 1927.

sage quoted from a contemporary criticism in *The Daily Telegraph* :

It was as if the record of those brilliant Shakespearean seasons at the old Lyceum, extending over a period of years, had been compressed into two brief hours, and memory flew back to the days when Henry Irving and Ellen Terry reigned supreme at that theatre, and by their marvellous art created a gallery of portraits which no one who had the privilege of looking upon will ever permit to lapse into oblivion.

The critic of *The Times* probed Ellen Terry's achievement more deeply, I think, showing its value to the new generation that had grown up since the Lyceum days, when he wrote :

It is a happy thing for England as well as for Miss Terry that she has found so effective a way of bringing home to Shakespeare's country men and women the inner meaning of his plays and the charm of her own art.

' Blow that word charm ! ' Ellen Terry often said after reading criticisms of her performance. ' There is something more in my acting than *charm*.' So it may have been a greater pleasure to her to read these words by another critic about her lecture on the heroines she styled ' Triumphant ' :

The Recital showed how much brainwork a great actress puts into her study of a part. Take all the

'triumphant' women Miss Terry dealt with—
Beatrice, Rosalind, Volumnia, Portia—when you
have heard what she has to say about the character of
each one, you will realize how poor your conception
of them was, compared with what she reveals to you.

This brainwork Ellen Terry put with indefatigable
industry, not only into the composition of these lectures, but into their delivery. Nearly every line in the
copy she most frequently used is annotated by some
instruction to herself about the way it should be
spoken. 'Take time.' 'Quiet.' 'Keep still.' 'Low
voice—almost intone—grave, solemn.' 'With humour,
rather reckless.' 'Ingratiating, irritating, babyish.'
'Horror, *not* loud.' 'Dark, fierce, violent.' 'Rather
cross.' 'Quick and quiet.' 'Whisper.' I opened a
page at random, a page in her study of Juliet, and from
it have transcribed these stage directions. On the flyleaf there are some general reflections which may help
the reader to conceive how the words of the lecture,
like the words in the scenes introduced, were vivified
when they were spoken by Ellen Terry.

Get the words into your remembrance first of all.
Then, (as you have to convey the meaning of the words
to *some* who have ears, but don't hear, and eyes, but
don't see) put the words into the simplest vernacular.
Then exercise your judgment about their sound.

So many different ways of speaking words ! Be
ware of sound and fury signifying nothing. Voice
unaccompanied by imagination, dreadful. Pom
posity, rotundity.

Imagination and intelligence absolutely necessa
to realize and portray high and low imagining .
Voice, yes, but not mere voice production. You m t
have a sensitive ear, and a sensitive judgment of e
effect on your audience. But all the time you must e
trying to please *yourself*.

Get yourself into *tune*. Then you can let fly y ur
imagination, and the words will seem to be supp ed
by yourself. Shakespeare supplied by oneself ! O !

Realism ? Yes, if we mean by that real feeling, real
sympathy. But people seem to mean by it onl the
realism of low-down things.

To act, you must make the thing written your wn.
You must steal the words, steal the thought, and *onvey*
the stolen treasure to others with great art.

It has often been remarked that Ellen Terry spoke
the language of Shakespeare as if it were her native
tongue, and in these communings with herself here is
revealed something of the process by wh ch she
arrived at that state of grace in which his words became her words.

His world too became her world : she was entirely
at home in it, as these lectures alone are left to testify
now that she is dead. She speaks in one of them of

its being ' more real to some of us than the actual world ', but I have never met anyone as familiar with it and its inhabitants as she. She lived on the most intimate terms with Shakespeare's men and women, and was always discovering something new about their idiosyncrasies. She told Henry Irving once that Shakespeare was the only man she had ever really loved. ' When I was about sixteen or seventeen, and very unhappy, I forswore the society of men. . . . Yet I was lonely all the same. I wanted a sweetheart. Well, Shakespeare became my sweetheart ! I read everything I could get hold of about my beloved one. I lived with him in his plays.'

It was undoubtedly a great grief to Ellen Terry to be prohibited at last from collaborating with her sweetheart in the theatre. Acting, from whatever it proceeds, goes back at last to the body. The body of this actress remained beautiful in age, but it could not be the body of Juliet or of any of Shakespeare's youthful heroines. Ellen Terry was happy in finding in these lectures a means of presenting women she could no longer represent, of showing what a lifelong study of them had taught her about their attributes. The opinion expressed by Bernard Shaw in his preface to *Ellen Terry and Bernard Shaw : A Correspondence* that Ellen Terry ' could do without the stage both as artist and woman' seems to me, who know how she hungered for it during the last twenty years of her life, to be ill-founded. The hunger was appeased to some extent by the opportunities for acting the lectures gave her.

What impression they will make on a reader who never saw Ellen Terry act I find it hard to conjecture. My share in their composition hinders me from expressing a disinterested opinion of their merits. I may be wrong in thinking that Ellen Terry hits the right nail on the head every time when she is analysing Shakespeare's characters, and giving her views about their impersonation in the theatre. Her comments on the characters of Juliet, Desdemona and Cordelia seem to me particularly good examples of her penetrating insight. They should do much to destroy the accepted notions of these characters, and induce actresses to abandon the traditional way of playing them.

The proof that Ellen Terry herself was never satisfied with the lectures lies in her unremitting efforts during ten years to improve them. She told me once she feared her revisions of the text had made them ' dreadfully patchy '. It was in this critical mood that she wrote under the title of the lecture on the Pathetic Heroines : ' Shreds and Patches '. Thereby hangs a rather amusing tale. One of her numerous volunteer and amateur secretaries inserted this sub-title in the matter for a handbill, announcing that she was going to lecture at the Hampshire House Club. I have a copy of this handbill preserved by Ellen Terry as a curiosity. ' Ellen Terry ' (in huge type) ' has consented to give a discourse on Shakespeare's Heroines :

' Shreds and Patches.'

' *What* a name for the poor ladies ! ! ' is the comment in Ellen Terry's writing.

To help the reader to see and hear her breathing into these ' shreds and patches ' the life which quickened the blood of her audiences I insert a vivid description of one of her lectures which she herself prized. She cut it out of the journal in which it appeared and pasted it on to the flyleaf of her most richly annotated copy of ' The Pathetic Heroines', with the note ' This is very good.' (The description refers, however, to the lecture on ' The Triumphant Heroines '.) On the same flyleaf is the inscription, a beautiful specimen of Ellen Terry's beautiful handwriting : ' Gloria in altissimis Deo, et in terra pax hominibus bonae voluntatis.' Was this the way Ellen Terry got herself ' into tune ' for the lecture ? I like to think so.

Miss Ellen Terry in her day has played many parts, but it is questionable if she ever found rôle more fitting

than that which she assumed so easily and successfully
last night. It in a sense epitomized these others, and
further permitted full and free play for her own win-
some and magnetic personality. Interesting and
illuminating as was the lecture, one discovered the
chiefest charm in the lecturer. The dark green hang-
ings and the lighting arrangements threw into relief all
the play of her mobile features ; her robes of crimson
fell into easy-flowing lines with each graceful gesture
of her eloquent hands. Her voice possesses still much
of the power and clarity of youth, and carried convincing proof of the yet youthful spirit. There was much
of eloquent suggestion in her visible appreciation of
the graciously accepted flowers ; in the manner in
which she swung a chair into position ; in her turning
over of the written pages on her lectern. Her asides
and impromptus were as pregnant with intention as
her set speeches.

She is speaking of the German Shakespearean
theatres enthusiastically, and then, her eye penetrating
the empty dimness of the hall, she adds with playful
irony : ' To which the people flock and flock.' It is
interesting to hear one who has taken part with Irving
in sumptuous Shakespearean revivals dismiss super-
fluous *dramatis personæ* as ' Lords, attendants and all
that sort of thing.' She is quick to seize on a platform
palm as a suitable hiding place for Beatrice in her delightful reading of the garden scene. ' You see that it is
a bower ? ' And her hearers did, succumbing readily
to the old hypnotic scenery of Globe Theatre days.

'I never could endure a reading of a character which entailed a sacrifice of beauty,' she says, and then naïvely to an applauding audience : 'I'm glad you think so too.' She is confidential, and informs us that she is partly Irish, partly Scottish, and that she is sure the Scottish part takes care of the Irish.

There is nothing conventional about her method or her matter. Of the scene between Benedick and Beatrice in church, she remarks : 'I intended to skip it ; I think now I'll read it.' Which she does to the great beatitude of her hearers. Continually in her illustrative acting she visualises memories of old Lyceum days, and bygone performances of Shakespearean heroines whom she herself made truly triumphant. In the brief hours one has the compressed and fragrant essence of a whole Shakespearean season. What could be finer than the contrast she suggested between Virgilia and Volumnia in the scene from *Coriolanus*? What could be more delightful than her reading of the Falstaffian love-missives received by Mistress Ford and Mistress Page unless it were to have been present at that memorable representation of these same merry wives by Mrs. Kendal and Ellen Terry herself? What could be more fitting than the note on which she closed in her wonderful declamation of Portia's eloquent appeal, which as the actress finely phrased it 'is in spirit as beautiful as the Lord's Prayer on which indeed it is modelled'?

The lecture was marked with much literary style ; it was full of little points of illumination not only of the Shakespearean text itself, but of the actress's method of approaching it. We may congratulate Miss Terry on having discovered so effective a method of conveying to her audiences the inner meaning of the Shakespearean plays ; her audiences may congratulate themselves that the method promises the great actress still a very considerable future among them.

The word abideth. I am hopeful that the publication of these lectures, even though they are only the scenarios of the plays Ellen Terry acted on stage and platform, promises her a future far more considerable than this writer prophesied. They may be read long after all who heard them have vanished from the earth.

CHRISTOPHER ST. JOHN

NOTE

ELLEN TERRY made her own ' acting version ' of the scenes from Shakespeare's plays interpolated in her lectures, and it has not been altered. The text is based for the most part on the Globe Edition.

THE CHILDREN IN SHAKESPEARE'S PLAYS

THE CHILDREN IN SHAKESPEARE'S PLAYS

WHEN the project of my giving some lectures on Shakespeare was first discussed, it occurred to me that as I had begun life as an actress by impersonating one of the children in his plays there would be something appropriate in my beginning life as a lecturer with a discourse on the subject of these children. The idea attracted me all the more strongly, because they have not been studied as exhaustively as their elders. In the course of a long life, many hours of which have been spent poring over the guide-books to that imaginary world of Shakespeare's, more real to some of us than the actual world, I have come across only the briefest references to the children. How many can you claim to know intimately? Forgive my putting this question, inspired by the confession of a friend, when I told her the subject I had in mind for my first lecture, that the only child in Shakespeare she could remember was Arthur in *King John*. 'The child who had his eyes put out,' she added, a proof that even her memory of Arthur was rather dim!

You are amused, and I have no doubt you can all do better than that. Still I am hopeful of being able to make your knowledge of Shakespeare's little boys deepen and glow. Yes, nearly all his children are of the male sex, one obvious reason for his predilection for it being the number of well-trained boy actors available for children's parts. There was in the Elizabethan theatre, as Rosencrantz tells Hamlet, ' an aery of children, little eyases that cry out on the top of question, and are most tyrannically clapped for it.' That ' sense of idiosyncratic character ', which Mr. Bernard Shaw, who as you know is no bardolater, considers one of Shakespeare's greatest assets as a dramatist, is as manifest in his children as in his adults. But no more clearing of the throat. ' Shall we clap into 't roundly, without hawking or spitting or saying we are hoarse, which are the only prologues to a bad voice ? ' That suggestion made by one of the young pages who sing that lovely ditty ' It was a lover and his lass ' in the Forest of Arden, ought to be acted upon by all speakers and lecturers.

So let me ' clap into ' Mamillius, little Prince Mamillius, son and heir to Leontes, King of Sicilia, in whose palace *The Winter's Tale* begins.

It is fifty years ago and more since I made my first appearance on the stage as Mamillius. When I spoke as a child and thought as a child I wonder whether I was able to reveal all I see now in this lovely child's part. The saying that the child is father to the man throws light on it. It is easy to recognise in Mamillius that imaginative, philosophic, poetic temperament which in its maturity is so frequently studied by Shakespeare. In his childish treble he pipes a few notes of the music poured out in profuse strains by Romeo and Hamlet. Try and imagine them when they were children. You will see little boys very like Mamillius.

' Come, my gracious lord, shall I be your play-fellow ? ' says one of his mother's ladies-in-waiting.

Visualise the scene. The royal mother is ill and tired. She has complained that the child ' so troubles me 'tis past enduring.' Her ladies must amuse him, satisfy his need for someone to play with.

Mamillius
No, I'll none of you.

First Lady
Why, my sweet lord ?

Mamillius
You'll kiss me hard and speak to me as if
I were a baby still. I love *you* better.

Second Lady
And why so, my lord ?

Mamillius

                Not for because
Your brows are blacker ; yet black brows they say
Become some women best, so that there be not
Too much hair there, but in a semicircle
Or a half-moon made with a pen. . . .

Second Lady

                     Who taught you this ?

Mamillius

  I learnt it out of women's faces.

Then he turns to the lady who speaks to him as if he were ' a baby still ' :

' What colour are *your* eyebrows ? ' Her reply ' Blue, my lord ' strikes me as one of those feeble jests some adults wrongly think will ' amuse the children '. Mamillius is not amused. He rebukes the lady for trying to fool him.

Nay, that's a mock. I have seen a lady's nose
That has been blue, but not her eyebrows.

An observant and wise babe ! We may assume that when his mother was barred from his presence ' like one infectious ' it was impossible to throw dust in his eyes. There are lines which prove that he is conscious of the reason. He may be too young to realize the nature of the charge his madly jealous father, the victim

28

of ' fancies too weak for boys, too green and idle for girls of nine ', has brought against his mother, but he knows she is in disgrace and he takes it terribly to heart.

> He straight declined, drooped, took it deeply,
> Fastened and fixed the shame on't in himself,
> Threw off his spirit, his appetite, his sleep,
> And downright languished.

In Swinburne's Study of Shakespeare, there is a lovely passage about Mamillius which I must read to you. The happy ending to *The Winter's Tale* could not console Swinburne for his loss.

' I have in me', he writes, ' so much of the spirit of Rachel weeping in Ramah as will not be comforted because Mamillius is not. It is well for those whose hearts are light enough to take comfort in the substitution of his sister Perdita for the boy who died of " thoughts high for one so tender ".'

These words, I should remind you, occur in Paulina's speech describing the death of the young Prince. Paulina, Hermione's champion, is quite sure he died of a broken heart :

> Whose honourable thoughts,
> Thoughts high for one so tender, cleft the heart
> That could conceive a gross and foolish sire
> Blemished his gracious dam.

'Even in her daughter's embrace', Swinburne goes on, 'it seems hard if his mother should have utterly forgotten the little voice that had only time to tell her just eight words of that ghost story which neither she nor we were ever to hear ended. . . . Anyone but Shakespeare would have sought to make pathetic profit out of the child by the easy means of showing him, if but once again, as changed and stricken for want of his mother. . . . Shakespeare only could find a better way, a subtler and deeper chord to strike, by giving us our last glimpse of him as he laughed and chattered with her " past enduring " . . . It may be that we remember him all the better because his father whose jealousy killed him, and his mother for love of whom he died, would seem to have forgotten the little brave sweet spirit.'

The glimpse we get of Mamillius with Leontes is enough to make us feel that the child is puzzled by his father's attitude to him, and rather scared. He does not chatter spontaneously, but answers the questions put to him in a few mechanically dutiful words.

'Mamillius, art thou my boy?' 'Ay, my good lord.' 'How now, you wanton calf! Art thou my calf?' 'Yes, if you will, my lord.' Why these questions? Leontes, tortured by jealousy, is observing Hermione and Polixenes all the time he asks them.

The suspicion his wife is unfaithful now breeds another. She may have been unfaithful before. What if Mamillius is not his son?

> . . . They say we are
> Almost as like as eggs : women say so,
> That will say any thing.

Affection for the child struggles with this monstrous suspicion.

> Come, sir page,
> Look on me with your welkin eye : sweet villain,
> Most dear'st ! my collop ! Can thy dam ?—may't
> be ?—

Then the unhappy man is reassured :

> Looking on the lines
> Of my boy's face, methought I did recoil
> Twenty-three years, and saw myself unbreeched
> In my green velvet coat . . .
> How like, methought, I then was to this kernel,
> This squash, this gentleman.

That was the time when Leontes and Polixenes, brought up together, were close friends. ' We were,' Polixenes tells Hermione, as ' twinned lambs that did frisk i' the sun.'

> Two lads that thought there was no more behind
> But such a day tomorrow as today,
> And to be boy eternal.

We learn in the first scene of the play that their friendship had outlasted their boyhood. Separated by ' royal necessities', one becoming King of Bohemia, the other, King of Sicily, they had kept up a correspondence and sent one another presents. Who could have foreseen that when these friends met again as men, they would soon become enemies ? Beware the green-eyed monster indeed ! It gets such a grip of Leontes that within a few weeks of Polixenes' arrival at his court he is planning to kill him.

Polixenes is vaguely aware of some hostility in his friend's attitude. ' My favour here begins to warp ', he says. That is the real reason for his anxiety to cut his visit short, although he pleads that his affairs drag him homeward. Hermione, urged by Leontes to press him to stay, makes light of this excuse. Find a better one ! Tell us you are longing to see your son again, and we shall have to let you go !

How Polixenes adores this son, Florizel, who is about the same age as Mamillius, we know from the answer he makes to Leontes' question :

Are you so fond of your young prince as we
Do seem to be of ours ?

Polixenes   If at home, sir,
He's all my exercise, my mirth, my matter.

Now my sworn friend, and then mine enemy,
My parasite, my soldier, statesman, all ;
He makes a July's day short as December,
And with his varying childness cures in me
Thoughts that would thick my blood.

It is pure conjecture, but I think reasonable conjecture, that Shakespeare in these lines is describing what his son Hamnet meant to him. And I believe that the grief he felt when Hamnet died is reflected in the passionate lamentations of Constance in *King John* over the loss of her only son. Those who have attempted to compare the order of the plays with the order of those events in Shakespeare's life which are reported, if not authenticated, tell us that shortly before writing *King John* Shakespeare had visited Stratford for the first time after ten years' absence. We may assume that then he learned to know and love Hamnet, and that Arthur, who is not in the least like the Arthur in the historical play from which *King John* was adapted, was studied from the life. If so, Hamnet was a singularly tender, unselfish and sweet-natured boy. When Arthur is taken prisoner, his first thought is of his mother :

' O, this will make my mother die with grief ! '
And indeed the news does nearly kill her, makes of her
' a grave unto a soul : holding the eternal spirit against

C

33

her will in the vile prison of afflicted breath.' This vehement, intemperate, ambitious Constance expresses her grief with a violence which justifies Cardinal Pandulph's rebuke : 'Lady, you utter madness and not sorrow.'

This steadies her for a moment. We hear her now speaking more calmly, quietly and slowly, and are more deeply moved :

> Thou art not holy to belie me so :
> I am not mad ; this hair I tear is mine :
> My name is Constance ; I was Geffrey's wife ;
> Young Arthur is my son, and he is lost :
> I am not mad : I would to heaven I were !
> For then 'tis like I should forget myself :
> O, if I could, what grief should I forget !
> Preach some philosophy to make me mad
> And thou shalt be canonized, Cardinal.
>
> .   .   .   .   .
>
> If I were mad I should forget my son,
> Or madly think a babe of clouts were he :
> I am not mad.

There is none of the ' unadvised scold ', as Queen Elinor calls Constance, in this pathetic speech, nor in the one inspired by King Philip's sarcastic remark that the distraught mother is as fond of grief as of her child.

> Grief fills the room up of my absent child,
> Lies in his bed, walks up and down with me,

Puts on his pretty looks, repeats his words,
Remembers me of all his gracious parts,
Stuffs out his vacant garments with his form ;
Then, have I reason to be fond of grief ?
Fare you well : had you such a loss as I,
I could give better comfort than you do.

The mother, I think, felt the separation more poignantly than the son. Arthur speaks of the grief it will cause her, but never of missing her, of longing to see her again. They have little in common, the ambitious worldly woman, stirring up everyone to support her son's claim to the throne, and the diffident unworldly boy who does not think he is worth the ' coil that's made for me ', who says he would be as merry as the day is long ' so I were out of prison and kept sheep '. Constance's bitter tongue makes Arthur wince. ' Peace ! ' he pleads, when she is rude to those she suspects of treachery to his cause.

' Come to thy grandam, child ', says Queen Elinor, in the scene in which John is bargaining with Arthur's supporters, promising to compensate the young prince if his claim to the throne is abandoned.

' Do, child ', says Constance jeeringly.

' Go to it grandam, child.
Give grandam kingdom, and it grandam will
Give it a plum, a cherry and a fig !
There's a good grandam ! '

'Good my mother, peace!' And as Arthur says this he bursts into tears. 'His mother shames him so, poor boy, he weeps.' This remark of Elinor's enrages Constance, and leads to fresh recriminations. The two queens quarrel with a violence which fully accounts for poor little Arthur's piteous wish that he were 'low laid' in his grave.

The scene between Hubert and Arthur in the prison is one of the best-known scenes in the plays. Probably all of you learned it by heart when you were children. As Shakespeare says in one of his sonnets: 'Things grown common lose their dear delights', and this beautiful scene may have lost some of its power to move you because it is hackneyed. This has not been my experience, however. I find it more poignant as the years go on, and have cried over it many times since the day I first cried over it when I was rehearsing the part of Arthur with Mrs. Charles Kean. She grew so angry with me because I failed again and again to show the anguish of Arthur when the executioners enter with the cord to bind him, and the irons to put out his eyes, that she gave me a good hard slap! Then real tears poured from my eyes, and my voice was shaken with sobs as I pleaded with Hubert to drive the men away. 'That's right! That's the way!' Mrs. Kean shouted in a great state of excitement. 'Good child! Now remember what you did with your voice . . . remember everything, and do it again ! ' I did not need another slap to make me cry . . . I thought : ' Red hot irons in my eyes would hurt far more.' This was my first lesson in using my imagination. I was taught that day that if we would express emotion naturally in the supernatural language of great dramatic poetry, we must first imagine the emotion in our own terms. Take care of the truth in Shakespeare's lines, and the poetry will take care of itself.[1]

Before we take leave of Arthur, who does not live long after Hubert has spared him, leaping to his death from the high wall of the castle when he is attempting to escape, let us consider what a rare character Shakespeare has created in him : an angelically good little boy who is not a prig ! Swinburne, who wrote such touching words about Mamillius, confessed that he could say nothing about Arthur. ' I am not minded to speak of him. There are one or two figures in the world of Shakespeare's work of which there are no words that would be fit or good to say. The place they have in our lives and thoughts is not one for talk.' So as he lies on the stones beneath the castle wall, com-

[1] Extracts from the scene between Hubert and Arthur are given in some of the texts of this lecture, but as Ellen Terry seldom read them, they have been omitted here.—C. St. J.

mending his soul to heaven, let us say no more than 'Good-night, sweet prince, and flights of angels sing thee to thy rest.'

Arthur, as I have suggested, may have had an original in Shakespeare's boy Hamnet. Perhaps little Will Page in *The Merry Wives of Windsor* is a sketch of Shakespeare himself in his youth. I feel that Shakespeare was thinking of his efforts to learn Latin at the grammar school at Stratford when he wrote that delightful scene in which Mrs. Page is taking her boy to school, and on the way meets his schoolmaster, Sir Hugh Evans. All the Latin phrases introduced are to be found, I am told, in the grammar which Shakespeare must have used. A very droll scene it is. Mrs. Page insists, as there is no school to-day (Master Slender having secured the boys a holiday), on Sir Hugh's putting Will a few questions in his 'accidence'. 'My husband says my son profits nothing in the world at his book.' Will might well be put off by the frequent interruptions of Mrs. Quickly, the village gossip, who makes some highly ingenious guesses at the meaning of the Latin words, but he keeps his head, and does well enough to justify his mother's remark : 'He is a better scholar than I thought he was.'

Shakespeare left school when he was still very young—at thirteen it is said. What did he do then ?

It is all conjecture. We may guess, if it pleases us, that he knocked about, doing odd jobs, picking up some knowledge of the world. It is quite possible that as in that little ' grammar ' scene in *The Merry Wives of Windsor* Shakespeare was drawing on his memories of his schooldays, so in other scenes in the same play in which Robin, Sir John Falstaff's page, plays a part, he was using some of his own experiences after he left school and ran wild.

We know from a passage in *Henry IV* that it was Prince Hal who got Robin his job with Falstaff, but we learn nothing of the boy's antecedents. There is a suggestion that he was not born in the gutter in the statement that Falstaff had the boy Christian, and ' look if the fat villain have not transformed him ape '. Yet he exhibits the precocity of the guttersnipe who almost from infancy has had to shift for himself. I figure him an undersized, wizened little creature, for children must have plenty of sleep, and plenty of good nourishing food to be well-grown, chubby-faced and plumplimbed. Robin's life with Sir John and his boon companions, a roystering lot, could not have been good for his health. But it appears to have sharpened his wits. He knows how to ingratiate himself with the ladies. The merry wives, Mrs. Page and Mrs. Ford, who draw him into their conspiracy to fool his master, both take to him. They are amused at the self-assurance of the ragged little imp, who pays them compliments like a grown-up gallant. 'How now, my eyas-musket, what news with you?' says Mrs. Ford, or to translate her greeting into language more familiar to you: 'Hullo, you little cock-sparrow, what have you been up to!' 'My master, Sir John', replies the cock-sparrow, 'is come in at your back door, Mistress Ford, and requests your company.'

Mrs. Page
    You little Jack-a-Lent, have you been true to us?

Robin
    Ay, I'll be sworn. My master knows not of your being here, and hath threatened to put me into everlasting liberty if I tell you of it; for he swears he'll turn me away.

Mrs. Page
    Thou'rt a good boy: this secrecy of thine shall be a tailor to thee and shall make thee a new doublet and hose.

If Falstaff had found out that his page was the merry wives' accomplice in making a fool of him, it is doubtful whether he would have turned him away, for this smart little lad was very useful to him. One of his jobs is to do the fat knight's shopping. We hear of his being commissioned to go to Master Dombledon's shop and buy satin for Falstaff's new short cloak and slops. The wily Master Dombledon refuses to give Falstaff credit, and Robin comes back without the satin :

'He said, sir, you should procure him better assurance than Bardolph. He would not take his bond and yours. He liked not the security.'

It is in this scene, which you will find in *Henry IV, Part II*, that Falstaff tells Robin that if Prince Hal put him into his service for any other reason than ' to be set off, why then I have no judgment'. Falstaff can always see a joke at his own expense. Does he not boast that he is not only witty in himself, ' but the cause that wit is in other men '? So he knows what the Prince was up to when he gave him this little snippet of a page. What a funny pair they would make ! The contrast in size would be a fresh source of inspiration to the men of all sorts who take a pride in girding at the fat knight ! But no one gets more fun out of the contrast than the fat knight himself. 'I do here walk before thee like a sow that hath overwhelmed all her litter but one.' ' Thou whoreson mandrake, thou art fitter to be worn in my cap than to wait at my heels.' And so on.

Robin has other qualifications for being Falstaff's page than that of ' setting him off ' physically. He is an alert and resourceful boy, and serves his master well. His loyalty to him is proved, in spite of those occasions when he joins in the sport of ragging him, by the fact that he does not desert him when he is down and out. Robin remains in Falstaff's service until his death. By that time the boy has seen a great deal of the seamy side of life. His schoolroom is the Boar's Head Tavern, his schoolmasters are drunkards and wastrels. He is encouraged by them to swagger and be impudent. When he makes fun of Bardolph's red nose, a standing joke in Falstaff's set, he is applauded and given money.

' A' calls me e'en now, my lord ', he tells Prince Hal, ' through a red lattice, and I could discern no part of his face from the window. At last I spied his eyes, and methought he had made two holes in the ale-wife's new petticoat, and so peeped through.' The Prince is delighted. ' Has not the boy profited ? '

Bardolph is ' asking for it ', I feel, when he tells his young tormentor to shut up.

' Away, you whoreson upright rabbit, away ! '

' Away, you rascally Althaea's Dream, away ! ' Robin retorts.

Now where did he pick up that name for Bardolph ? From his master, I expect. It is new to the Prince.

42

'Instruct us, boy. What dream, boy?'

'Marry, my lord, Althaea dreamed she was delivered of a firebrand, and therefore I call him her dream.'

The Prince
A crown's worth of good interpretation. There 'tis, boy.

Poins
O that this good blossom could be kept from cankers! Well, there is sixpence to preserve thee.

Five-and-six, a big sum in those days, for cheeking Bardolph! Well, who would grudge it to Robin? I am sure he needed the money, for Sir John did not pay his wages regularly, and let him go about in rags. Bardolph's comment, 'An you do not make him hanged among you, the gallows shall have wrong', is none the less pertinent. If the boy had not had his head screwed on the right way he might have deteriorated in such company and come to a bad end. But, as we find out later on (in *Henry V*), he sees through his associates, and has too much contempt for them to make them his model.

Frightened as he is when Falstaff is taken ill, not knowing what to do for him, and rushing off to Pistol and his wife (our old friend Mrs. Quickly) for help, he doesn't forget to tease Bardolph :

' Mine host Pistol, you must come to my master, and you, hostess.   He is very sick, and would to bed. ...Good Bardolph, put thy face between his sheets and do the office of a warming pan.   Faith, he's very ill.'

Mrs. Quickly-Pistol runs off at once, and, like Robin, is alarmed at poor old Sir John's condition.   In the street outside her tavern, the old gang are brawling as usual.   The quarrel this time is about eight shillings Pistol owes Nym.   It becomes so fierce that swords have been drawn by the time Mrs. Quickly comes back, and begs them to come in to Sir John.

' Ah, poor heart ! he is so shaked of a burning quotidian tertian that it is most lamentable to behold. Sweet men, come to him.'

The next thing we hear about Sir John is that he is dead.   There they all are sitting outside the tavern, his friends and his boy, each one mourning his loss, for each one in his way loved the fat knight.   It is a wonderful scene, rich in implications.   It is surely one that Robin has for the time lost his pert, confident manner, and is looking what he feels, a forlorn little boy without a friend in the world, in Pistol's words : ' Boy, bristle thy courage up.'   I think they are all grateful to Pistol for breaking the gloomy silence. They find it a relief to talk about the dead man. But better I should read you the scene than describe it.

Bardolph
    Would I were with him wheresome'er he is, either in heaven or in hell !

Mrs. Quickly
    Nay, sure, he's not in hell : he's in Arthur's bosom, if ever man went to Arthur's bosom. A' made a finer end and went away an it had been any christom child : a' parted even just between twelve and one, even at the turning o' the tide : for after I saw him fumble with the sheets and play with flowers and smile upon his fingers' ends, I knew there was but one way ; for his nose was as sharp as a pen, and a'babbled of green fields. ' How now, Sir John ! ' quoth I : ' what, man ! be o' good cheer.' So a' cried out ' God ! God ! God ! ' three or four times. Now I, to comfort him, bid him a' should not think of God : I hoped there was no need to trouble himself with any such thoughts yet. So a' bade me lay more clothes on his feet : I put my hand into the bed and felt them, and they were as cold as any stone ; then I felt to his knees, and they were as cold as any stone ; and so upward and upward, and all was as cold as any stone.

Nym
    They say he cried out of sack.

Mrs. Quickly
Ay, that a' did !

Bardolph
And of women.

Mrs. Quickly
Nay, that a' did not !

Robin
Yes, that a' did ; and said they were devils incarnate.

Mrs. Quickly
A' could never abide carnation : 'twas a colour he never liked.

Robin
Do you not remember, a' saw a flea stick upon Bardolph's nose, and a' said it was a black soul burning in hell-fire ?

Bardolph
Well, the fuel is gone that maintained that fire : that's all the riches I got in his service.

The old Falstaff gang go off to the war in France, and their conduct at the front makes Robin ashamed of being their 'boy'. In the scene before Harfleur when they have to be hounded to the attack, we hear his candid opinion of Nym, Bardolph and Pistol :

As young as I am, I have observed these three swashers. I am boy to them all three, but all they three, though they would serve me, could not be man to me, for indeed three such antics do not amount to a man. For Bardolph, he is white-livered and red-faced, by the means whereof a' faces it out, but fights not. For Pistol, he hath a killing tongue and a quiet sword, by the means whereof a' breaks words and keeps whole weapons. For Nym, he hath heard that men of few words are the best men, and therefore he scorns to say his prayers, lest a' should be thought a coward. But his few bad words are matched with as few good deeds : for a' never broke any man's head but his own, and that was against a post when he was drunk. . . . Nym and Bardolph are sworn brothers in filching. . . . They would have me as familiar with men's pockets as their gloves or their handkerchers, which makes much against my manhood. . . . I must leave them, and seek some better service ; their villany goes against my weak stomach and therefore I must cast it up.

Sensible boy ! But he finds it difficult to break with his old associates, his sole legacy from Falstaff, and get another job. He is still with Pistol when the English army are at Agincourt. It never seems to occur to him to try and get into touch with the King who in his wild Prince Hal days employed him. Perhaps he is deterred from the attempt by the memory of that dreadful day when Sir John had met the King coming from his coronation, and the King had snubbed his master, pretending at first that he did not know him. For a moment Robin had thought it might be only a joke. How often the prince had played such tricks on Falstaff ! But he had never seen the prince look like this before. That cold haughty stare made Robin uncomfortable. And when the prince spoke, his words and his manner left no doubt at all that he was in earnest :

> I know thee not, old man : fall to thy prayers :
> How ill white hairs become a fool and jester !
> I have long dreamd of such a kind of man,
> So surfeit-swell'd, so old and so profane,
> But, being awaked, I do despise my dream.
>
> .   .   .   .   .
>
> Reply not to me with a fool-born jest :
> Presume not that I am the thing I was :
> For God doth know, so shall the world perceive,
> That I have turned away my former self ;
> So will I those that kept me company.

It was in vain after that for poor old Sir John to try and bluff Robin and the others with the assurance that 'he would be sent for in private', that 'the King must seem thus to the world.' They knew the truth. After Falstaff's disgrace, it is doubtful whether any one of them would have dared to approach the King and beg a favour of him for the sake of old times.

Hardly has Robin made up his mind to leave the

' three swashers ' when two of them, Nym and Bardolph, are hanged. And so would Pistol be, in Robin's
comment, ' if he durst steal anything adventurously.'
The last time we see the boy, he is in Pistol's company
acting as interpreter between that bragging rascal and
a French prisoner. Robin's French is quite fluent. Did
he learn to speak the lingo from Prince Hal, or from
Falstaff in London, or did he pick it up during his few
weeks in France with the army ? I am curious about
everything that concerns this child for whom I have
a great affection. It makes me sad that he should be
denied the chance of that ' better service' to which he
aspires, and be killed at Agincourt while in the rear
minding the baggage. His remark that the ' French
might have a good prey of it ', if they knew of it, ' for
there is none to guard it but boys ', is characteristic of
the sharp-witted youngster. He is always alert and
observant.

Allowing that the English, as he implies, were careless, this massacre of the innocents seems to me none
the less a disgraceful business. I share the indignation
of the Welsh commander, Fluellen, with the cowardly
rascals, the refuse of the French army, who were guilty
of it.

' Kill the poys and the luggage ! 'Tis expressly
against the law of arms : 'tis as arrant a piece of

knavery, mark you now, as can be offer't : in your
conscience, now, is it not ? '

Gower agrees and adds that it's certain there's not a
boy left alive. These ' glorious dead ' are not men-
tioned by King Henry when he reads out the Agincourt roll of honour. ' None else of name ' on that
roll, he says, after Edward Duke of York, the Earl of
Suffolk, Sir Richard Ketly and Davy Gam, Esquire.
It seems hard that the King should never know that
the boy he put in Falstaff's service died in his own.
Poor little chap ! Fame, which after his first experience
of fighting he says he would give ' for a pot of ale and
safety ', is denied him at the end.

The majority of little boys have a natural tendency
to militarism, and in young Marcius, the son of the
great Roman soldier Coriolanus, it has been encouraged by his grandmother Volumnia, who boasts
that if she had a dozen sons, she would rather eleven
died for their country than one ' voluptuously surfeit
out of action '. The child, too, we are expressly told,
has inherited his father's qualities. He does not favour
his mother, the gentle timid Virgilia, who is too acutely
sensitive to the horrors of war to take pride in the
heroism of soldiers. She is not as glad as Volumnia
that Marcius would ' rather see the swords and hear a

drum than look upon his schoolmaster '. I imagine that she looks distressed when their neighbour, the Lady Valeria, who has called on them bursting with the latest news from the front, tells the story of Marcius and the butterfly :

> O' my word, the father's son : I'll swear 'tis a very pretty boy. O' my troth, I looked upon him o' Wednesday half an hour together : has such a confirmed countenance. I saw him run after a gilded butterfly : and when he caught it, he let it go again ; and after it again ; and over and over he comes, and up again : catched it again ; or whether his fall enraged him, or how 'twas, he did so set his teeth and tear it : O, I warrant how he mammocked it !

' One on's father's moods ', says Marcius's proud grandmother exultantly. His mother's comment : ' A crack, madam ', suggests that she thinks his exhibition of childish temper is nothing to boast about, rather something to be apologised for, on the ground of thoughtless youth. ' Crack ' here is used in the Elizabethan sense of ' mischievous boy '.

Marcius speaks for himself only once in the play ; he is a very important figure in the action all the same, most important of all on that memorable day when Volumnia dresses him in a mourning habit, and leads him forth with his mother and the Lady Valeria, and other great ladies of Rome (all in mourning too), to the place outside the walls where the Volscians are encamped. I should perhaps remind you what is the object of this journey. Coriolanus, having quarrelled with the Roman tribunes, has been banished, and is now returning to take vengeance on his own countrymen with the aid of a foreign army, the very army he had defeated once in the service of Rome. His friend Menenius has pleaded with him in vain to spare the city. Volumnia's intercession is its last hope. Probably little Marcius is too young to understand the situation. All he knows is that they are going to see father, and beg him not to do something shameful and wrong. His grannie has told him to be a good boy, and not forget to kneel down when she speaks to father.

So far we may imagine. Now let us come to the reality, described in Shakespeare's most magnificent manner. Coriolanus, who has turned a deaf ear to the appeal of Menenius, and told him harshly that his wife, his mother, and his child now mean nothing to him, is deeply moved when they appear before him.

> My wife comes foremost ; then the honour'd mould
> Wherein this trunk was framed, and in her hand
> The grandchild to her blood. But, out, affection !
> All bond and privilege of nature, break !

          . . . My mother bows,
As if Olympus to a molehill should
In supplication nod : and my young boy
Hath an aspect of intercession, which
Great nature cries, 'Deny not'.   Let the Volsces
Plough Rome, and harrow Italy !   I'll never
Be such a gosling to obey instinct, but stand
As if a man were author of himself
And knew no other kin.

Virgilia

          My lord and husband !

Coriolanus
These eyes are not the same I wore in Rome.

Virgilia
The sorrow that delivers us thus changed
Makes you think so.

Coriolanus
          Like a dull actor now,
I have forgot my part, and I am out,
Even to a full disgrace.   Best of my flesh,
Forgive my tyranny ; but do not say
For that 'Forgive our Romans.'

Coriolanus embraces his wife, mingling endearing
words with his kisses.   Then he becomes suddenly and
sharply conscious that he has taken no notice of his
mother :
          You gods ! I prate,
And the most noble mother of the world

Leave unsaluted ; sink, my knee, i' the earth ;
Of thy deep duty more impression show
Than that of common sons.

Volumnia

O, stand up blest !
Whilst, with no softer cushion than the flint,
I kneel before thee. . . .

She draws his attention to Valeria, and while he is
saluting her, pushes forward little Marcius :

This is a poor epitome of yours,
Which by the interpretation of full time
May show like all yourself.

Coriolanus

The god of soldiers,
With the consent of supreme Jove, inform
Thy thoughts with nobleness ; that thou mayst
prove
To shame unvulnerable, and stick i' the wars
Like a great sea-mark, standing every flaw,
And saving those that eye thee !

Volumnia

Your knee, sirrah !

Poor Marcius ! He has forgotten all about that
kneeling business, and I imagine he blushes and nearly
cries with confusion when his grannie gives him a
shove to remind him. Surely it is to cheer him up

and help him to keep back his tears that his father says
'That's my brave boy!' Having got Marcius on to
his knees according to plan, Volumnia goes on:

> Even he, your wife, this lady, and myself
> Are suitors to you.

Coriolanus
> I beseech you, peace:
> Or if you'ld ask, remember this before:
> The thing I have forsworn to grant may never
> Be held by you denials. Do not bid me
> Dismiss my soldiers, or capitulate
> Again with Rome's mechanics: tell me not
> Wherein I seem unnatural; desire not
> To allay my rages and revenges with
> Your colder reasons.

Volumnia
> O, no more, no more!
> You have said you will not grant us any thing:
> For we have nothing else to ask, but that
> Which you deny already: yet we will ask;
>
> .   .   .   .   .
>
> Should we be silent and not speak, our raiment
> And state of bodies would bewray what life
> We have led since thy exile. Think with thyself
> How more unfortunate than all living women
> Are we come hither; since that thy sight, which
>   should
> Make our eyes flow with joy, hearts dance with
>   comforts,

Constrains them weep and shake with fear and
    sorrow ;
Making the mother, wife and child to see
The son, the husband and the father tearing
His country's bowels out. . . .
               We must find
An evident calamity, though we had
Our wish, which side should win ; for either thou
Must, as a foreign recreant, be led
With manacles through our streets, or else
Triumphantly tread on thy country's ruin,
And bear the palm for having bravely shed
Thy wife and children's blood.

At that word ' tread ', young Marcius sets his teeth
as on the day he mammocked the butterfly.

             A' shall not tread on *me* ;
  I'll run away till I am bigger, but then I'll fight!

This pathetic little outburst of pugnacity, with its
touch of the discretion which is the better part of
valour, affects Coriolanus more than his mother's
taunts and his wife's tears. He feels himself to be
weakening, and with the words ' I have sat too long ',
rises to go away. Volumnia is quick to notice his
emotion, and presses her advantage. Her arguments
become more forcible, her words more eloquent :

             Thou know'st, great son,
The end of war's uncertain, but this certain,

That, if thou conquer Rome, the benefit
Which thou shalt thereby reap is such a name,
Whose repetition will be dogg'd with curses ;
Whose chronicle thus writ : ' The man was noble,
But with his last attempt he wiped it out ;
Destroyed his country, and his name remains
To the ensuing age abhorr'd '.   Speak to me, son.

  . . . . .

        Why dost not speak ?
Think'st thou it honourable for a noble man
Still to remember wrongs ?   Daughter, speak you :
He cares not for your weeping.   Speak thou, boy :
Perhaps thy childishness will move him more
Than can our reasons.   There's no man in the
  world
More bound to's mother ; yet here he lets me prate
Like one i' the stocks ! Thou hast never in thy life
Show'd thy dear mother any courtesy,
When she, poor hen, fond of no second brood,
Has clucked thee to the wars and safely home,
Loaden with honour.   Say my request's unjust,
And spurn me back ; but if it be not so,
Thou art not honest . . .
       He turns away :
Down, ladies : let us shame him with our knees.
    . . . Down ! An end :
This is the last : so we will home to Rome,
And die among our neighbours.   Nay, behold's :
This boy, that cannot tell what he would have,
But kneels, and holds up hands for fellowship,

Does reason our petition with more strength
Than thou hast to deny't.

Once more Volumnia depends on young Marcius
to conquer Coriolanus. Still he holds out, and now
she speaks daggers, barbed with irony :

Come, let us go !
This fellow had a Volscian to his mother ;
His wife is in Corioli, and his child
Like him by chance !

Coriolanus is stung to the quick by this contemptuous speech, but he says nothing. What indeed is
there for him to say ? He can only make a gesture of
entreaty to his mother to stop. At least this is the
inference to be drawn from her next words :

Yet give us our dispatch :
I am hush'd until our city be afire
And then I'll speak a little.

At that he takes her hand, and according to one of
Shakespeare's rare stage directions, ' holds it, silent '.
She has prevailed, but, as he tells her after his first
agonized cry : ' O mother, mother, what have you
done ? ', most dangerously. She has saved Rome, but
at the price of her son's life.

We get a glimpse of another child in *Macbeth*. The
scene in which he appears is so often omitted from

acting versions of the play that you may never have
seen it. I had not, until last year when the Elizabethan Stage Society produced *Macbeth* in its entirety.
Those who cut the scene may plead that it is not of
great importance in the action, but it is so vividly
human that it is a shame to deprive audiences of it.
The child, who is not given a name in the list of characters, but described simply as ' Boy, son to Macduff ',
must be made incarnate in the theatre for us to realize
how wonderfully he is made. Before I let him speak
for himself (unlike young Marcius he is very talkative)
I should like to conjure up the situation in which we
meet him. Lord Ross has come to tell Lady Macduff
that her husband has fled into England. She knows
nothing of the cause of his flight, and resents his having
left her and her young children unprotected in a lonely
castle in Fife in these bad troublous times.

Lady Macduff
What had he done, to make him fly the land ?

Ross
You must have patience, madam.

Lady Macduff
                    He had none :
His flight was madness : when our actions do not,
Our fears do make us traitors.

Ross
>   You know not
>   Whether it was his wisdom or his fear.

Lady Macduff
>   Wisdom ! to leave his wife, to leave his babes,
>   His mansion and his titles in a place
>   From whence himself does fly ? He loves us not :
>   He wants the natural touch : for the poor wren,
>   The most diminutive of birds, will fight,
>   Her young ones in her nest, against the owl.
>   All is the fear and nothing is the love ;
>   As little is the wisdom, where the flight
>   So runs against all reason.

Ross
>   My dearest coz,
>   I pray you, school yourself : but for your husband,
>   He is noble, wise, judicious, and best knows
>   The fits o' the season. I dare not speak much
>   further ;
>   . . . I take my leave of you :
>   Shall not be long but I'll be here again :
>   Things at the worst will cease, or else climb upward
>   To what they were before.   My pretty cousin,
>   Blessing upon you !

Lady Macduff
>   Father'd he is, and yet he's fatherless.

Ross
>   I am so much a fool, should I stay longer,
>   It would be my disgrace and your discomfort :
>   I take my leave at once.

He goes away, and Lady Macduff, after seeing him out, begins to talk with her boy ; a little boy, I think, not more than five years old :

Lady Macduff
>   Sirrah, your father's dead :
> And what will you do now ? How will you live ?

Son
> As birds do, mother.

Lady Macduff
>   What, with worms and flies ?

Son
> With what I get, I mean, and so do they.

Lady Macduff
> Poor bird ! thou'ldst never fear the net nor lime,
> The pitfall nor the gin.

Son
> Why should I, mother ?   Poor birds they are not
>   set for.
> My father is not dead, for all your saying.

Lady Macduff
> Yes, he is dead : how wilt thou do for a father ?

Son
> Nay, how will you do for a husband ?

Lady Macduff
> Why, I can buy me twenty at any market.

Son
Then you'll buy 'em to sell again.

Lady Macduff
Thou speak'st with all thy wit.

Her son is indeed a sharp-witted child, not easily bluffed. There has been something in his mother's voice and manner which has made him doubt that his father is dead. Now he expresses a doubt that she is just to him :

Son
Was my father a traitor, mother ?

Lady Macduff
Ay, that he was.

Son
What is a traitor ?

Lady Macduff
Why, one that swears and lies.

Son
And be all traitors that do so ?

Lady Macduff
Every one that does so is a traitor, and must be hanged.

Son
And must they all be hanged that swear and lie ?

Lady Macduff
Every one.

Son

Who must hang them?

Lady Macduff

Why, the honest men.

Son

Then the liars and swearers are fools, for there are liars and swearers enow to beat the honest men and hang up *them*.

Lady Macduff

Now, God help thee, poor monkey! But how wilt thou do for a father?

Son

If he were dead, you'd weep for him; if you would not, it were a good sign that I should quickly have a new father.

Lady Macduff

Poor prattler, how thou talk'st.

Poor prattler! In a few minutes his clever tongue is silenced for ever. It is the last and perhaps the worst of Macbeth's crimes—this brutal murder of Lady Macduff and her innocent babes. Well may Macduff say when the news reaches him:

> Did Heaven look on
> And would not take their part?

The young Princes in *Richard III* are, I think, more widely known than any of Shakespeare's children except Prince Arthur. Yet the difference in their characters may not have struck everyone who has read or seen the play. The elder brother, Prince Edward (that same prince of history who had such a tragically brief reign as Edward V) gives the impression, thanks to Shakespeare's skill in revealing character in a few strokes, of being a serious-minded, studious boy, with quiet dignified manners. He is a great contrast to Prince Richard, Duke of York, a smart, lively child with a clever but rather pert tongue. It is York whom we meet first in the play, in company with his grandmother, the Duchess of York, his mother, the widowed Queen of Edward IV, and Archbishop Rotherham. The elder Prince is not present. He is on his way, travelling from Ludlow to London for his coronation. The Archbishop speaks :

> Last night, I hear, they lay at Northampton ;
> At Stony-Stratford will they be tonight :
> Tomorrow, or next day, they will be here.

Duchess of York
> I long with all my heart to see the prince :
> I hope he is much grown since last I saw him.

The Queen
> But I hear, no : they say my son of York
> Hath almost overta'en him in his growth.

York

Ay, mother ; but I would not have it so.

Duchess

Why, my young cousin, it is good to grow.

York

Grandam, one night as we did sit at supper,
My uncle Rivers talk'd how I did grow
More than my brother : ' Ay ', quoth my uncle
    Gloucester,
' Small herbs have grace, great weeds do grow
    apace.'
And since, methinks, I would not grow so fast,
Because sweet flowers are slow and weeds make
    haste.

Duchess

Good faith, good faith, the saying did not hold
In him that did object the same to thee :
He was the wretched'st thing when he was young,
So long a-growing and so leisurely,
That, if this rule were true, he should be gracious !

Archbishop

Why, madam, so, no doubt, he is.

Duchess

I hope he is, but yet let mothers doubt.

York

Now, by my troth, if I had been remember'd,
I could have given my uncle's grace a flout,
To touch his growth nearer than he touch'd mine.

Duchess
How, my pretty York ? I pray thee, let me hear it.

York
Marry, they say my uncle grew so fast
That he could gnaw a crust at two hours old :
'Twas full two years ere I could get a tooth.
Grandam, this would have been a biting jest.

Duchess
I pray thee, pretty York, who told thee this ?

York
Grandam, his nurse.

Duchess
His nurse ! why, she was dead ere thou wert born.

York
If 'twere not she, I cannot tell who told me.

Queen
A parlous boy : go to, you are too shrewd.

Archbishop
Good madam, be not angry with the child.

The Queen
Pitchers have ears.

We get the impression from this vivid little scene—
such a good scene to act—that York is the kind of boy
who takes a delight in pulling his elders' legs !

His brother is not that kind. I can't imagine his
wishing he had seized an opportunity to make a

'biting jest' at his uncle's expense! When we first see him, he looks grave and thoughtful. He has a great deal on his mind besides his approaching coronation, an ordeal for a boy of thirteen. The arrest of his favourite uncles—his mother's brothers, Lord Rivers and Lord Grey—has been a shock to him. He is beginning to doubt the good faith of his other uncle, Richard, and is not to be bluffed by Richard's assumption of affection. This is all false, Edward thinks, when Richard says :

> Welcome, dear cousin, my thoughts' sovereign :
> The weary way hath made you melancholy.

The boy answers coldly :

> No, uncle ; but our crosses on the way
> Have made it tedious, wearisome, and heavy :
> I want more uncles here to welcome me.

Richard tries again :

> Sweet prince, the untainted virtue of your years
> Hath not yet dived into the world's deceit :
>   .   .   .   .   .
> Those uncles which you want were dangerous ;
> Your grace attended to their sugar'd words,
> But look'd not on the poison of their hearts :
> God keep you from them, and from such false
>   friends !

The Prince looks at him searchingly : and with the contemptuous exclamation, ' God keep me from false

friends ! but they were none,' turns away to greet the
Lord Mayor, who has come to receive him on his
entry into London.   Later in the scene he again manifests his distrust of Richard :

> Say, uncle Gloucester, if our brother come,
> Where shall we sojourn till our coronation ?

Gloucester
> Where it seems best unto your royal self.
> If I may counsel you, some day or two
> Your highness shall repose you at the Tower :
> Then where you please, and shall be thought most fit
> For your best health and recreation.

Prince
> I do not like the Tower, of any place.
> Did Julius Caesar build that place, my lord ?

The ' lord ' he addresses now is my lord of Buckingham, who is in the conspiracy to put Gloucester on the
throne.

Buckingham
> He did, my gracious lord, begin that place ;
> Which, since, succeeding ages have re-edified.

Prince
> Is it upon record, or else reported
> Successively from age to age, he built it ?

Buckingham
> Upon record, my gracious lord.

Prince
> But say, my lord, it were not register'd,
> Methinks the truth should live from age to age,
> As 'twere retail'd to all posterity,
> Even to the general all-ending day.

' So wise so young, they say, do never live long,'
his uncle mutters under his breath, and the Prince is not
too much absorbed in his conversation with Buckingham to notice it :

Prince
> What say you, uncle ?

Gloucester
> I say, without characters, fame lives long.

The Prince appears to be satisfied that this is what
Gloucester said, but I think he keeps his eye on him, as
he expresses the opinion that it is the word which gives
life to fame.

> That Julius Caesar was a famous man ;
> With what his valour did enrich his wit,
> His wit set down to make his valour live :
> Death makes no conquest of this conqueror ;
> For now he lives in fame, though not in life.
> I'll tell you what, my cousin Buckingham,—

Buckingham
> What, my gracious lord ?

Prince
    An if I live until I be a man,
    I'll win our ancient right in France again,
    Or die a soldier, as I lived a king !

Buckingham
    Now, in good time, here comes the Duke of York.

The Princes greet one another.   Notice that York, a born tease, immediately quizzes his brother about his new dignity.

Prince
    Richard of York ! how fares our loving brother ?

York
    Well, my dread lord ; so must I call you now.

Prince
    Ay, brother, to our grief, as it is yours :
    Too late he died that might have kept that title,
    Which, by his death, hath lost much majesty.

Gloucester
    How fares our cousin, noble Lord of York ?

York
    I thank you, gentle uncle.   O, my lord,
    You said that idle weeds are fast in growth :
    The prince, my brother, hath outgrown me far.

Gloucester
    He hath, my lord.

York

And therefore is he idle?

Gloucester
O, my fair cousin, I must not say so.

York
Then he is more beholding to you than I.

Gloucester
He may command me as my sovereign,
But you have power in me as in a kinsman.

York
I pray you, uncle, give me this dagger.

Gloucester
My dagger, little cousin? With all my heart.

Prince
A beggar, brother?

Forgive me for interrupting the scene here to emphasise the necessity, when reading a play, of trying to visualise it in action. Our success will depend on the amount of study we give the lines. The greater the dramatist the richer his lines in *implications*. What is the implication when the Prince says ' A beggar, brother?' Surely that he thinks York is behaving with a lack of dignity, and must be stopped. A further implication, suggesting what we players call 'business', is that York thinks his brother rather dense not to dis-

cern that his begging is only a mock. I imagine that
he gives Edward a warning wink, or nudge—some
signal to shut up ! At any rate Edward does shut up
and York goes on 'ragging' uncle Gloucester for a
time unrebuked :

Prince
  A beggar, brother ?

York
  Of my kind uncle, that I know will give,
  And being but a toy, which is no grief to give.

Gloucester
  A greater gift than that I'll give my cousin.

York
  A greater gift ! O, that's the sword to it !

Gloucester
  Ay, gentle cousin, were it light enough.

York
  O, then, I see, you will part but with light gifts ;
  In weightier things you'll say a beggar nay.

Gloucester
  It is too heavy for your grace to wear.

York
  I weigh it lightly, were it heavier.

Gloucester
  What, would you have my weapon, little lord ?

York
  I would, that I might thank you as you call me.

Gloucester
  How ?

York
  Little.

At this Edward breaks silence. Perhaps he sees
that York has gone too far, that his impertinence has
made their uncle really angry.

Prince
  My Lord of York will still be cross in talk :
  Uncle, your grace knows how to bear with him.

York
  You mean, to bear me, not to bear with me :
  Uncle, my brother mocks both you and me ;
  Because that I am little, like an ape,
  He thinks that you should bear me on your shoulders.

This sally certainly justifies Buckingham's comment :

  With what a sharp-provided wit he reasons !
  To mitigate the scorn he gives his uncle,
  He prettily and aptly taunts himself ;
  So cunning and so young is wonderful !

Richard has had enough of ' little prating York '
and his bold, quick, ingenious taunts. He hurries the
Princes off to the Tower, not without a protest from

York, who in this as in everything, proves he is much
sharper than his brother :

York
  What, will you go unto the Tower, my lord ?

Prince
  My lord protector needs will have it so.

York
  I shall not sleep in quiet at the Tower.

Gloucester
  Why, what should you fear ?

York
  Marry, my uncle Clarence' angry ghost ;
  My grandam told me he was murder'd there.

Prince
  I fear no uncles dead.

Gloucester
  Nor none that live, I hope.

Prince
  An if they live, I hope I need not fear.
  But come, my lord : and with a heavy heart,
  Thinking on them, go I unto the Tower.

Although the men who were hired to murder the
Princes are described as ' flesh'd villains, bloody dogs ',
they could not speak of their deaths without weeping.

74

There they lay asleep, ' girdling one another within their innocent alabaster arms '.   A book of prayers lay on the pillow, which, said Forest, one of the murderers, ' almost changed my mind '.   His fellow, Dighton, seeing him weaken, seized the pillow and pressed it down on the children's lips.   That is all we are told, I am thankful to say.   Tyrrel, from whom we hear of the murder, spares us horrible details, and is lavish with beautiful ones such as :

Their lips were four red roses on a stalk
Which in their summer beauty kissed each other.

I think now I have presented all the children of whom Shakespeare makes a separate study.   We hear of a lovely Indian boy, the cause of all the trouble between Titania and Oberon in *A Midsummer Night's Dream* ; we see Queen Elizabeth as a baby at her christening in *Henry VIII.*, and Perdita as a baby, left by Antigonus, either for life or death, in a desert country near the sea. . . .   Then there is Moth, Armado's page in *Love's Labour's Lost*, a ' well-educated infant ', as his master calls him, but a little too precocious for my taste.   What a clever answer he makes when he is asked how he has purchased his experience. ' By my penny of observation '.   That explains well enough how Shakespeare gained his knowledge of children. He was a keen observer of human beings at all ages, ' from the infant muling and puking in the nurse's arms ', to ' the lean and slippered pantaloon with spectacles on nose ', piping and whistling in a voice ' turning again to childish treble '.

THE TRIUMPHANT WOMEN

THE TRIUMPHANT WOMEN

' ONE said it thundered ; another that an angel spake '.
There you have in a nutshell the great mass of literature on the subject of Shakespeare ! What more
natural than that students of his plays should arrive at
such a variety of conclusions about them ? Don't we
all see in any work of art what we bring to it ? We
can't avoid bringing what is part and parcel of ourselves, temperament and culture for instance, but we
can, if we will, leave behind such things as theories,
preconceived notions, prejudices, and predilections.
When we approach Shakespeare, whether in the
theatre or in the class-room or in the library, we should
certainly leave behind any rigid theory we may have
formed, or picked up ready-made, for there is a danger
of our trying to shrink or stretch everything, scenes,
characters and lines, to fit it. I know this from experience. When I was preparing this lecture, I soon
realised that all Shakespeare's heroines could not be
discussed in it, even in the most superficial way ; I

79

should have to devote two lectures at least to them. This involved some sort of classification. The arrangement which seemed to me least arbitrary was to bring the happy women in the comedies together in one group, and make up the other of the sorrowful women in the tragedies. But no sooner had I stuck on the labels 'triumphant' and 'pathetic' than I felt this division into types was a mistake. Shakespeare's characters are far too idiosyncratic to fit this or that mould, and we can make them fit only by the process known as 'wangling'. I have kept my labels as a convenience, but you will find that in the 'pathetic' group there are women who have nothing more in common than a tragic fate, and that the 'triumphant' group includes women of very different temperaments. Please don't think any 'theory' is implied in my classification. I leave theories to the scholars. An actress does not study a character with a view to proving something about the dramatist who created it. Her task is to learn how to translate this character into herself, how to make its thoughts her thoughts, its words her words. It is because I have applied myself to this task for a great many years, that I am able to speak to you about Shakespeare's women with the knowledge that can be gained only from union with them.

Wonderful women ! Have you ever thought how much we all, and women especially, owe to Shakespeare for his vindication of woman in these fearless, high-spirited, resolute and intelligent heroines ? Don't believe the anti-feminists if they tell you, as I was once told, that Shakespeare had to endow his women with virile qualities because in his theatre they were always impersonated by men ! This may account for the frequency with which they masquerade as boys, but I am convinced that it had little influence on Shakespeare's studies of women. They owe far more to the liberal ideas about the sex which were fermenting in Shakespeare's age. The assumption that ' the woman's movement ' is of very recent date—something peculiarly modern—is not warranted by history. There is evidence of its existence in the fifteenth century. Then as now it excited opposition and ridicule, but still it moved ! Such progress was made that Erasmus could write : ' Men and women have different functions, but their education and their virtues ought to be equal.' He was shocked at the ignorance of young ladies of rank in the Low Countries. They were not nearly as well educated as their contemporaries in France, Italy and England. The scholarship of Lady Jane Grey, who at thirteen could read Plato in the original ; of Mary Stuart, who at sixteen delivered an extempore

oration in Latin ; of Queen Elizabeth who made trans-
lations of the classics, was not exceptional in the class of
society which received any education at all. Vives,
the Spanish tutor of Katharine of Aragon, who accom-
panied her to England, urged, like Erasmus, that girls
should be given as good an education as boys. Then,
as now, some people thought this most undesirable.
What use was learning to a woman ? It might even
have the dreadful result of making her less attractive
to a man ! The masculine dislike of the intellectual woman is expressed by the critic of Vives who
wrote :

'From a braying mule and a girl who speaks Latin
good Lord deliver us ! '

That women were teased about wanting to ' wear
the breeches ' is clear from an Italian caricature, dated
1450, which represents some fashionable ladies of the
period struggling awkwardly to pull on men's trunk-
hose !

Much more could be said to emphasise the point
that the real women in Shakespeare's time inspired
his general conception of femininity, but I am conscious
that it is about time I ' cut the cackle ' and came to
' the 'osses ', that is, to Beatrice, Portia, and Rosalind,
and the other heroines in my ' triumphant ' group.
Yet there is one bit of cackle I am unwilling to sacrifice.

I must read a contemporary description of a great lady of the Renaissance period, Margaret of France, because it might have been written about Shakespeare's Beatrice :

' Her eyes are clear, and full of fire ; her mouth is fine—intellectual with something of irony, of benevolence, and of reserve. A singular countenance where the mind and the heart both rule.'

Beatrice to the life ! Her brilliant mind has a strong deep heart for its consort. Her cousin Hero criticises her for being too much under the sway of her mind :

> Her wit
> Values itself so highly that to her
> All matter else seems weak.

Her uncle Leonato endorses this criticism when he tells Beatrice that she will never get a husband if she is so shrewd of her tongue. Yet when her heart speaks seriously, Beatrice listens seriously and obeys its commands.

' By my troth a pleasant-spirited lady ', says Don Pedro. The actress who impersonates Beatrice should remember that testimonial. Beatrice's repartee in her encounters with Benedick can easily be made to sound malicious and vulgar. It should be spoken as the lightest raillery, with mirth in the voice, and charm in the manner. An ounce of practice is worth a pound of theory, so I will read one of the scenes in which the merry lady Beatrice and the merry gentleman Benedick cut and thrust at one another, making several palpable hits. The teasing merry lady begins the verbal fencing bout :

I wonder that you will still be talking, Signior Benedick : nobody marks you.

Benedick
What, my dear Lady Disdain, are you yet living ?

Beatrice
Is it possible disdain should die while she hath such meet food to feed it as Signior Benedick ! Courtesy itself must convert to disdain if you come in her presence.

Benedick
Then is courtesy a turncoat. But it is certain I am loved of all ladies, only you excepted ; and I would I could find in my heart that I had not a hard heart ; for truly I love none.

Beatrice
A dear happiness to women : they would else have been troubled with a pernicious suitor. I thank God, and my cold blood, I am of your humour for that : I had rather hear my dog bark at a crow than a man swear he loves me.

Benedick

God keep your ladyship still in that mind : so some gentleman or other shall 'scape a predestinate scratched face.

Beatrice

Scratching could not make it worse, an 'twere such a face as yours.

Benedick

Well, you are a rare parrot-teacher.

Beatrice

A bird of my tongue is better than a beast of yours.

Benedick

I would my horse had the speed of your tongue, and so good a continuer ! But keep your way i' God's name. I have done !

Beatrice

You always end with a jade's trick. I know you of old.

The result of this duel is a draw. Another, conducted in masks during a revel at Leonato's house, ends in a victory for Beatrice. She is in particularly good form that night, ' huddling jest upon jest ', says her victim, ' with such impossible conveyance upon me that I stood like a man at a mark with a whole army shooting at me '. The absurdity of the situation strikes Benedick's friend and prince, Don Pedro. Here are two people strongly attracted by one another, and unwilling to admit it, because both are afraid of the admission being laughed at. The scheme concocted by Don Pedro to get them out of their impasse is very ingenuous and simple, but not to be despised as it is successful. When a man and a woman are in this position : 'Does she love me ? I don't know.' 'Does he love me ? I don't know ', they need a Don Pedro to clear up the matter. He has the wit to see that Beatrice is the wife for Benedick, and Benedick the husband for Beatrice. 'I would fain have it a match, and I doubt not but to fashion it, if you three ' (he is speaking to Beatrice's uncle Leonato, her cousin Hero, and Hero's Claudio who is going to be married to her the next day) ' will but minister such assistance as I shall give you direction.'

Don Pedro either gave better ' direction ' to Hero, or she carried out his plan better, for her way of working on Beatrice is far more intelligent than the men's way of working on Benedick. The stories which Benedick, hidden in the arbour, hears them tell of Beatrice's passion for him are so absurd that it is surprising he does not suspect a trick. The conversation between Hero and Ursula which Beatrice overhears has a more genuine ring. It seems quite natural that Beatrice should take it seriously, and be convinced that

Benedick loves her, but is determined not to give her a chance of mocking at his love.   Beatrice is proud, but not vain.   It is because she is not vain that she recognises the element of truth in what Hero and Ursula say about her.

Hero
>   . . . She cannot love,
> Nor take no shape nor project of affection,
> She is so self-endeared.

Ursula
>   Sure I think so ;
> And therefore certainly it were not good
> She knew his love, lest she make sport at it.

Hero
> Why, you speak truth.   I never yet saw man,
> How wise, how noble, young, how rarely featured,
> But she would spell him backward : if fair-faced,
> She would swear the gentleman should be her sister ;
> If black, why Nature, drawing of an antique,
> Made a foul blot !

.   .   .   .   .

> If speaking, why, a vane blown with all winds ;
> If silent, why, a block moved with none.
> So turns she every man the wrong side out.

.   .   .   .   .

Ursula
> Sure, sure, such carping is not commendable.

Hero
> No, not to be so odd and from all fashions
> As Beatrice is, cannot be commendable ;
> But who dare tell her so ?   If I should speak
> She would mock me into air.

And much besides. When the conspirators have
finished and gone their ways, satisfied that they have
limed the bird, according to Don Pedro's instructions,
Beatrice comes forward and unpacks her heart in
words.   Very difficult words for an actress ; not very
effective, but charged with the passion of a strong, deep
heart !   I have played Beatrice hundreds of times and
never done this speech as I feel it should be done :

> What fire is in mine ears ?   Can this be true ?
> Stand I condemn'd for pride and scorn so much ?
> Contempt, farewell, and maiden pride, adieu !
> No glory lives behind the back of such !
> And, Benedick, love on.   I will requite thee,
> Taming my wild heart to thy loving hand.
> If thou dost love, my kindness shall incite thee
> To bind our loves up in a holy band ;
> For others say thou dost deserve, and I
> Believe it better than reportingly.

Nevertheless if Benedick had failed Beatrice when
she denounces his friend Claudio for the infamous
charge he brings against Hero at their wedding, for
which she would have Benedick punish him even with

death, she would have cast him out of her heart. 'If you are not for me you are against me, and the man who is against me in this is not the man for me', is implied in everything Beatrice says to Benedick in the church scene.

Notice that all the men, except the Friar, are inclined to think there must be something in Claudio's accusation ! Even Hero's father, Leonato, asks whether it is likely that Claudio, who loved her so that 'speaking of her foulness' he 'washed it with tears', is lying. Even Benedick is so 'attired in wonder', he doesn't know what to say. The evidence that Hero has a lover, that on the eve of her wedding she was with him, is given by men for whom Benedick has respect and affection. If Don Pedro and Claudio are mistaken, they must be the victims of some diabolically ingenious plot. What more probable than that Pedro's brother John who detests Claudio is at the bottom of it ? Benedick's loyalty to his friends makes him anxious to find some excuse for them. His attitude is incomprehensible to Beatrice. He knows not what to say indeed ! In her opinion there is only one thing to be said, and blazing with indignation, she says it :

O on my soul, my cousin is belied !

There is only one thing to be done. The slanderer,

who has had the brutality to shame Hero in public, must be punished. That is a man's job, and Beatrice is deeply disappointed in Benedick for not volunteering for it. Instead he gives his support to the friar's scheme for bringing Claudio to repentance by giving out that Hero has ' died upon his words '.

This is the situation when Benedick and Beatrice are left alone together in the church. Let them now speak for themselves.[1]

Benedick
Lady Beatrice, have you wept all this while ?

Beatrice
Yea, and I will weep a while longer.

Benedick
I will not desire that.

Beatrice
You have no reason. I do it freely.

Benedick
Surely I do believe your fair cousin is wronged.

Beatrice
Ah, how much might the man deserve of me that would right her !

---

[1] On the margin of the page of the manuscript in which this scene occurs Ellen Terry flashed down the words ' Not *emotion*. A *passion* ' in the handwriting Bernard Shaw said ' is as characteristic and unforgettable as her face '.

Benedick
Is there any way to show such friendship ?

Beatrice
A very even way, but no such friend !

Benedick
May a man do it ?

Beatrice
It is a man's office, but not yours.

Benedick
I do love nothing in the world so well as you : is not that strange ?

Beatrice
As strange as the thing I know not. It were as possible for me to say I loved nothing so well as you : but believe me not ; and yet I lie not : I confess nothing, nor I deny nothing. I am sorry for my cousin.

Benedick
By my sword, Beatrice, thou lovest me.

Beatrice
Do not swear, and eat it.

Benedick
I will swear by it that you love me, and I will make him eat it that says I love not you.

Beatrice
Will you not eat your word ?

Benedick

With no sauce that can be devised to it. I protest I love thee.

Beatrice

Why then, God forgive me !

Benedick

What offence, sweet Beatrice ?

Beatrice

You have stayed me in a happy hour ! I was about to protest I loved you.

Benedick

And do it with all thy heart.

Beatrice

I love you with so much of my heart that none is left to protest.

Benedick

Come, bid me do anything for thee.

Beatrice

Kill Claudio.

Benedick

Ha ! not for the wide world !

Beatrice

You kill me, to deny it. Farewell.

Benedick

Tarry, sweet Beatrice.

Beatrice
I am gone, though I am here : there is no love in you : nay, I pray you, let me go.

Benedick
Beatrice—

Beatrice
In faith, I *will* go.

Benedick
We'll be friends first.

Beatrice
You dare easier be friends with me than fight with mine enemy.

Benedick
Is Claudio thine enemy ?

Beatrice
Is he not approved in the height a villain, that hath slandered, scorned, dishonoured my kinswoman ? O that I were a man ! What, bear her in hand until they come to take hands ; and then with public accusation, uncovered slander, unmitigated rancour, —O God, that I were a man ! I would eat his heart in the market-place !

Benedick
Hear me, Beatrice—

Beatrice
Talk with a man out at a window ! A proper saying !

93

Benedick
Nay, but Beatrice,—

Beatrice
Sweet Hero ! She is wronged, she is slandered, she is undone.

Benedick
Beat—

Beatrice
Princes and counties ! Surely a princely testimony, a goodly count ! Count Comfect ! A sweet gallant, surely ! O that I were a man for his sake, or that I had any friend would be a man for my sake ! But manhood is melted into courtesies, valour into compliment, and men are only turned into tongue, and trim ones too : he is now as valiant as Hercules that only tells a lie and swears it ! I cannot be a man with wishing ; therefore I will die a woman with grieving.

Benedick
Tarry, good Beatrice. By this hand, I love thee.

Beatrice
Use it for my love some other way than swearing by it.

Benedick
Think you in your soul the Count Claudio hath wronged Hero ?

Beatrice
Yea, as sure as I have a thought or a soul.

Benedick
Enough, I am engaged. I will challenge him. I will kiss your hand, and so I leave you. By this hand, Claudio shall render me a dear account. As you hear of me, so think of me. Go, comfort your cousin : I must say she is dead : and so farewell.

This wonderful scene throws such a flood of light on Beatrice's character that an actress has little excuse for not seeing clearly what kind of woman she has to impersonate. Yet however it may be now, there is evidence that in the past she was not taken seriously enough. Even in the church scene I have just read to you the idea was to make her indignation rather comic. When I first rehearsed Beatrice at the Lyceum I was told by Mr. Lacy, an actor of the old school who was engaged by Henry Irving to assist him in some of his early Shakespearean productions, of some traditional ' business ' which seemed to me so preposterous that I could hardly believe he really meant me to adopt it. But he was quite serious. ' When Benedick rushes forward to lift up Hero after she has fainted, you " shoo " him away. Jealousy, you see. Beatrice is not going to let her man lay a finger on another woman '. I said, ' Oh, nonsense, Mr. Lacy ! ' ' Well, it's always been done ', he retorted, ' and it always gets a laugh '. I told him then that not only was it impossible for *me* to do such a thing, but that it was so inconsistent with Beatrice's character that it ought to be impossible for any actress impersonating her to do it ! I came off victorious in that tussle with Mr. Lacy, but was defeated in another with Henry Irving over a traditional ' gag ' at the end of the church scene. I had omitted this gag, ' Kiss my hand again ', when I had first played Beatrice in the provinces, and I was appalled at finding that I was expected to say it at the Lyceum. My tongue refused to utter the obnoxious words, impossible to the Beatrice of my conception, for many rehearsals. Then one day Henry said : ' Now I think it is about time to rehearse this scene as we are actually going to play it, so, Miss Terry, we must please have the gag '. I did not like to show any insubordination before the company, so with a gulp, I managed to obey, but I burst into tears ! Henry was most sympathetic, I remember, but would not budge. I went home in a terrible state of mind, strongly tempted to throw up my part ! Then I reflected that for one thing I did not like doing at the Lyceum, there would probably be a hundred things I should dislike doing in another theatre. So I agreed to do what Henry wished, under protest.

I have played Beatrice hundreds of times, but not once as I know she ought to be played. I was never swift enough, not nearly swift enough at the Lyceum where I had a too deliberate, though polished and thoughtful Benedick in Henry Irving. But at least I did not make the mistake of being arch and skittish, and this encourages me to think I could have played Rosalind well.

I have been Beatrice ! Would that I could say ' I have been Rosalind '. Would that the opportunity to play this part had come my way when I was in my prime ! I reckon it one of the greatest disappointments of my life that it did not ! In my old age I go on studying Rosalind, rather wistfully, I admit.

A contemporary of Shakespeare's writes that ' those who are illustrious by long descent reveal their nobility beyond possibility of mistake. They have in them a simplicity, a naïve goodwill, a delicate good feeling that separate them from the arrogant assumptions or false noblesse '. Of such is Rosalind. She shows these qualities of the well-bred at all times, as unmistakably when ' caparisoned like a man ' she is roughing it in the Forest of Arden, as when in the dignified dress of a lady of rank she is leading a sheltered life at her uncle's court.

This uncle who has usurped her father's dukedom

has not exiled her with him, but kept her to be a companion to his daughter Celia. Rosalind has adapted herself to this subordinate position with a good grace. It has been made more tolerable by the devotion of Celia ; she does all she can to prevent her cousin from feeling the change in her circumstances. Her resignation to it annoys the Duke. He finds offence in the fact that she gives no offence. Of late, says one of the courtiers, Le Beau, he

> Hath ta'en displeasure 'gainst his gentle niece,
> Grounded upon no other argument
> But that the people praise her for her virtues
> And pity her for her good father's sake :
> And on my life his malice 'gainst the lady
> Will suddenly break forth.

It does, with a vengeance, in the scene I am going to read to you. It takes place in a room in the palace. The cousins and friends—they are what we should call now ' good pals '—enter, and from Celia's first words, we gather that there is something wrong with Rosalind to-day. She is in low spirits, and disinclined to talk. Since that wrestling match when a handsome youth threw the Duke's famous wrestler Charles, succeeding where hundreds of challengers had failed, Rosalind has had much to make her thoughtful. She has fallen in love at first sight. She is quite sure she has found her mate in the wrestler, whom she has identified as Orlando, the son of an old friend of her father's, yet the chances are against their meeting again. The Duke had shown his hostility to Orlando plainly enough. Rosalind reflects sadly how different things would be if this were still her father's palace. Then Orlando would be a welcome guest. However, she shakes off her depression when Celia rallies her (as I have already pointed out, she is well-bred), and is soon joking about her troubles :

Celia
Why cousin ! Why Rosalind ! Cupid have mercy ! Not a word ?

Rosalind
Not one to throw at a dog.

Celia
No, thy words are too precious to be cast away upon curs ; throw some of them at me : come, lame me with reasons. . . . Is all this for your father ?

Rosalind
No, some of it is for my child's father ! O, how full of briers is this working-day world !

Celia
They are but burs, cousin, thrown upon thee in holiday foolery ; if we walk not in the trodden paths, our very petticoats will catch them.

Rosalind
I could shake them off my coat : these burs are in my heart.

Celia
Hem then away.

Rosalind
I would try if I could cry ' hem ', and have him !

Celia
Come, come, wrestle with thy affections.

Rosalind
O, they take the part of a better wrestler than myself !

Celia
. . . But turning these jests out of service, let us talk in good earnest. Is it possible, on such a sudden, you should fall into so strong a liking with old Sir Rowland's youngest son ?

Rosalind
The Duke, my father, loved his father dearly.

Celia
Doth it therefore ensue that you should love his son dearly ? By this kind of chase, I should hate him, for my father hated his father dearly ; yet I hate not Orlando.

Rosalind
No, faith, hate him not, for my sake.

Celia
　　Why should I not ? doth he not deserve well ?

Rosalind
　　Let me love him for that : and do you love him be-
　　cause I do.　Look, here comes the duke.

Celia
　　With his eyes full of anger.

And the Duke comes blustering in, followed by
' lords, attendants ' and that sort of thing.　He is in a
great rage, all fuss and noise.　He speaks to Rosalind
in a bullying tone :

　　Mistress, dispatch you with your safest haste
　　And get you from our court.

Rosalind
　　　　　　　　Me, uncle ?

Duke Frederick
　　　　　　　　You, cousin ;
　　Within these ten days if that thou be'st found
　　So near our public court as twenty miles,
　　Thou diest for it.

Rosalind takes this threat with dignity.　She asks
gravely and quietly for an explanation :

　　　　　　　I do beseech your grace,
　　Let me the knowledge of my fault bear with me.
　　If with myself I hold intelligence,

Or have acquaintance with mine own desires,
If that I do not dream, or be not frantic,—
As I do trust I am not,—then, dear uncle,
Never so much as in a thought unborn
Did I offend your highness.

Duke Frederick

    Thus do all traitors ;
If their purgation did consist in words,
They are as innocent as grace itself.
Let it suffice thee that I trust thee not.

Rosalind

Yet your mistrust cannot make me a traitor.
Tell me whereon the likelihood depends.

Now this is exactly what the Duke cannot do. So beside himself with rage, the rage of a man who knows he is in the wrong, he bellows out :

Thou art thy father's daughter : there's enough.

Rosalind (*with a touch of irony*—my *stage direction this !*)

So was I when your highness took his dukedom :
So was I when your highness banish'd him.
Treason is not inherited, my lord ;
Or, if we did derive it from our friends,
What's that to me ?   My father was no traitor ;
Then, good my liege, mistake me not so much
To think my poverty is treacherous.

Then little Celia intervenes :

Celia
Dear sovereign, hear me speak.

Duke Frederick
Ay, Celia, we stay'd her for your sake ;
Else had she with her father ranged along.

Celia
I did not then entreat to have her stay ;
It was your pleasure, and your own remorse :
I was too young that time to value her ;
But now I know her : if she be a traitor,
Why, so am I : we still have slept together,
Rose at an instant, learn'd, play'd, eat together ;
And wheresoe'er we went, like Juno's swans,
Still we went coupled and inseparable.

.   .   .   .   .

Duke Frederick
Thou art a fool : she robs thee of thy name,
And thou wilt show more bright and seem more
    virtuous
When she is gone.   Then open not thy lips ;
Firm and irrevocable is my doom
Which I have pass'd upon her.   She is banish'd.

Celia
Pronounce that sentence then on me, my liege,
I cannot live out of her company.

The Duke is staggered at this.   He still thinks of his
little Celia as a child, and here she is standing up to him

without any childish fear. ' You are a fool ', he repeats. Then he turns to Rosalind, and threatens her
again :

> You, niece, provide yourself.
> If you outstay the time, upon mine honour,
> And in the greatness of my word, you die.

With this he blusters out of the room, furious that
Rosalind shows no signs of being intimidated. She
breaks down, however, when she is left alone with
Celia, and Celia puts her arms round her and tries to
comfort her.

Celia
I charge thee, be not thou more grieved than I am.

Rosalind
I have more cause.

Celia
> Thou hast not, cousin.
> Prithee, be cheerful : know'st thou not, the duke
> Hath banish'd me, his daughter ?

Rosalind (smiling now, I think)
> That he hath not.

Celia
No, hath not ? Rosalind lacks then the love
Which teacheth thee that thou and I am one :
Shall we be sunder'd ? shall we part, sweet girl ?

No ; let my father seek another heir.
Therefore devise with me how we may fly,
Whither to go, and what to bear with us.
And do not seek to take your change upon you,
To bear your griefs yourself and leave me out ;
For, by this heaven, now at our sorrows pale,
Say what thou canst, I'll go along with thee.

Rosalind
Why, whither shall we go ?

Celia
To seek my uncle in the forest of Arden.

Rosalind, the cleverer one of the two, had not
thought of this ! It does seem a good idea, but she
sees how difficult it will be to carry it out :

Alas, what danger will it be to us,
Maids as we are, to travel forth so far !
Beauty provoketh thieves sooner than gold.

Why that's nothing ! We can make ourselves look
ugly ! That, in plain prose, is what Celia says next :

I'll put myself in poor and mean attire,
And with a kind of umber smirch my face.
The like do you : so shall we pass along,
And never stir assailants.

Now they plan the whole thing out in a twinkling.
They have forgotten everything except what fun it will

be, and are in rollicking spirits ! Such is the resilience of youth.

Rosalind (*in great glee, I think*)
　　　　　　　Were it not better,
　　Because that I am more than common tall,
　　That I did suit me all points like a man ?
　　A gallant curtle-axe upon my thigh,
　　A boar-spear in my hand ; and—in my heart
　　Lie there what hidden woman's fear there will—
　　We'll have a swashing and a martial outside,
　　As many other mannish cowards have
　　That do outface it with their semblances.

Celia
　　What shall I call thee when thou art a man ?

Rosalind (*bursting with laughter, I think*)
　　I'll have no worse a name than Jove's own page ;
　　And therefore look you call me Ganymede.
　　But what will *you* be call'd ?

Celia
　　Something that hath a reference to my state :
　　No longer Celia, but Aliena.

Rosalind
　　But, cousin, what if we assayed to steal
　　The clownish fool out of your father's court ?
　　Would he not be a comfort to our travel ?

Celia
　　He'll go along o'er the wide world with me.

Leave me alone to woo him.   Let's away,
And get our jewels and our wealth together,
Devise the fittest time and safest way
To hide us from pursuit that will be made
After my flight.   Now go we in content
To liberty, and not to banishment !

So these gallant young things set off for the Forest
of Arden, a beautiful setting for the beautiful idyll of
Orlando and Rosalind, an idyll that begins in jest and
ends in the tenderest earnest.

I said at the beginning of this discourse that Shakespeare's characters are far too idiosyncratic to be
divided into types.   Yet it does strike us when we
become familiar with them that he has a predilection
for a certain kind of temperament.   The temperament
with which he most frequently endows his heroes is—
well I can find no better description of it than ' thoughtful '.   It is even more difficult to describe the temperament of his heroines.   The majority of them are
women of strong character, high-mettled, quick-
witted, and resourceful.   But Shakespeare's predilection for them did not prevent him from drawing with
equal skill women of a different temperament.   There
is no play which provides us with a better proof of this
than *Coriolanus*.   Coriolanus's timid, sensitive wife
Virgilia, filled with terror for his safety every time he

goes into action, is as masterly a creation as his lion-hearted, patriotic mother Volumnia.

We meet them first in Coriolanus's house. The great soldier is away, fighting the Volscian enemy, and they are sitting together, conversing over their sewing. Volumnia rebukes her daughter-in-law for being nervous and depressed :

I pray you, daughter, sing, or express yourself in a more comfortable sort : if my son were my husband, I should freelier rejoice in that absence wherein he won honour than in the embracements where he would show most love. When yet he was but tender-bodied, when youth with comeliness plucked all gaze his way, when for a day of kings' entreaties a mother should not sell him an hour from her beholding, I, considering how honour would become such a person, that it was no better than picture-like to hang by the wall, if renown made it not stir, was pleased to let him seek danger where he was like to find fame. To a cruel war I sent him ; from whence he returned, his brows bound with oak. I tell thee, daughter, I sprang not more in joy at first hearing he was a man-child than now in first seeing he had proved himself a man.

Virgilia
But had he died in the business, madam, how then ?

This question shows that poor Virgilia is not made

of the stuff of Roman matrons. Volumnia, who is,
replies :

> Then his good report should have been my son ;
> I therein would have found issue. Hear me profess
> sincerely : had I a dozen sons . . . I had rather had
> eleven die nobly for their country than one volup-
> tuously surfeit out of action.

A gentlewoman comes in and announces that the
Lady Valeria is come to visit them. To talk about the
war, Virgilia knows. It is the last straw.

' Beseech you ', she cries out in anguish, ' give me
leave to retire myself.'

' I never heard such nonsense ', Volumnia thinks,
and pushing Virgilia back into her seat, says sternly :
' Indeed you shall not.' Then, sniffing the news from
the front that Lady Valeria, always well-informed
about the war, has called to tell them, Volumnia breaks
into a gallop of rhetoric :

> Methinks I hear hither your husband's drum,
> See him pluck Aufidius down by the hair. . . .
> Methinks I see him stamp thus, and call thus :
> ' Come on, you cowards ! you were got in fear
> Though you were born in Rome ! ' His bloody
> > brow
> With his mail'd hand then wiping, forth he goes,
> Like to a harvest-man that's task'd to mow
> Or all or lose his hire.

Virgilia

His bloody brow ! O Jupiter, no blood !

Volumnia

Away, you fool ! It more becomes a man
Than gilt his trophy.

How true it all sounds, and how Roman ! Yet it
has been said that whether Shakespeare's scene is
Athens, Rome, Verona or Egypt, whether the period
is classical or renaissance, his characters are all English
and all Elizabethan. This very play *Coriolanus* is
quoted in evidence. Shakespeare makes a mob in
ancient Rome talk and behave like a mob in the
London of his own day. He did not see much difference between them. But was there so much ? Those
words, 'Was ever feather so lightly blown to and fro as
this multitude ', are surely true of the mob at all times
in all countries. But when Shakespeare is dealing with
individuals, he often shows remarkable insight into the
different temperaments of different races. You have
only to compare *The Merchant of Venice* with *The
Merry Wives of Windsor* to become convinced of this.

In *The Merry Wives* the characters really are Elizabethan and English. Shakespeare is studying his com-
patriots and contemporaries in this joyous farce. Here
is the English race in a holiday mood, enjoying itself
very much as it does now on a Bank Holiday. Mrs.

Page and Mrs. Ford in the same group as Volumnia !
That may seem odd to you, but after all I am talking of
' triumphant heroines ', and no one can deny that the
hoax these merry English wives carry out on the fat
knight, John Falstaff, is a triumph for them. The
characters of these two women are very different, as I
hope to demonstrate by reading you the scene in which
they decide to ' larn ' the amorous old ruffian that
wives can be merry, and yet honest too.

Mrs. Page comes on reading a love-letter from him :

Mrs. Page
What, have I scaped love-letters in the holiday-time
of my beauty, and am I now a subject for them ?
Let me see.

' Ask me no reason why I love you ; for though
Love use Reason for his physician, he admits him
not for his counsellor. You are not young, no more
am I ; go to, then, there's sympathy : you are
merry, so am I ; ha, ha ! then there's more sympathy : you love sack, and so do I ; would you
desire better sympathy ? Let it suffice thee, Mistress
Page,—at the least, if the love of soldier can suffice,—
that I love thee. I will not say, pity me ; 'tis not a
soldier-like phrase ; but I say, love me. By me,

> Thine own true knight,
> By day or night,
> Or any kind of light,

With all his might
For thee to fight.   JOHN FALSTAFF.'

O wicked, wicked world ! One that is well-nigh worn to pieces with age to show himself a young gallant ! What an unweighed behaviour hath this Flemish drunkard picked out of my conversation, that he dares in this manner assay me ? Why, he hath not been thrice in my company ! What should I say to him ? Why, I'll exhibit a bill in the parliament for the putting down of men. How shall I be revenged on him ? for revenged I will be, as sure as his guts are made of puddings !

Mrs. Page is interrupted at this point by Mrs. Ford, who comes on, all in a flutter, an open letter in her hand. I always see Mrs. Ford as a rather demure little body, less free and easy in her manners than Mrs. Page, yet with something in her eye which is distinctly coy, something which makes Mr. Ford's jealousy not altogether irrational. It is that ' something ' which accounts for Mrs. Ford's being rather flattered by Sir John's attentions. It is clear that she is disappointed when she finds he is paying them to Mrs. Page too.

But let us go back to the scene :

Mrs. Ford
Mistress Page ! trust me, I was going to your house.

Mrs. Page
And, trust me, *I* was coming to *you* ! You look very ill.

Mrs. Ford
Nay, I'll ne'er believe that ; I have to show to the contrary. O Mistress Page, give me some counsel !

Mrs. Page
What's the matter, woman ?

Mrs. Ford
O woman, if it were not for one trifling respect, I could come to such honour !

Mrs. Page
Hang the trifle, woman ! take the honour ! What is it ?—dispense with trifles—what is it ?

Mrs. Ford
If I would but go to hell for an eternal moment or so, I could be knighted.

Mrs. Page
What ! thou liest ! Sir Alice Ford ! . . .

Mrs. Ford
Here, read, read ! Perceive how I might be knighted ! Did you ever hear the like ? ' Thine own true knight.' I shall think the worse of fat men as long as I have an eye to make difference of men's liking. . . . ' By day or night.'

Mrs. Page
' Or any kind of light.'

Mrs. Ford
 ' With all his might.'

Both
 ' For thee to fight—John Falstaff.'

Mrs. Page
 Letter for letter, but that the name of Page and Ford differs ! To thy great comfort, here is the twin-brother of thy letter ! . . . I warrant he hath a thousand of these letters, writ with blank space for different names—sure more—and these are of the second edition : he'll print 'em !

Mrs. Ford (*rather disappointed, I think, as she compares the letters*)
 Why, this is the very same ; the very hand, the very words. What doth he think of us ?

Mrs. Page
 Nay, I know not ! . . . Let's be revenged on him : let's appoint him a meeting : give him a show of comfort in his suit, and lead him on with a fine-baited delay, till he hath pawned his horses to mine host of the Garter.

Mrs. Ford
 Nay, I will consent to act any villany against him, that may not sully the chariness of our honesty. O, that my husband saw this letter ! It would give eternal food to his jealousy !

Mrs. Page
 Why, look where he comes; and *my* good man too :

he's as far from jealousy as I am from giving him cause; and that, I hope, is an unmeasurable distance.

Mrs. Ford
You are the happier woman.

Mrs. Page
Let's consult together against this greasy knight ! Come hither !

And off they go, arm in arm, seething with plans for revenging themselves on Falstaff. If we followed them we should have some fun, broad Elizabethan fun—it might shock some of you—but time is short, and we have yet to go to Italy and meet Portia of Belmont.

No one can tell us how Shakespeare got what we call ' local colour '. He may have been to Italy. He may not. It is ' as you like it '. His Venetian topography is amazingly accurate, but that proves nothing. He could have got it out of a book, or picked it up from an Italian traveller he met in a coffee-house in London. It does not matter. What does matter is that the genius of the man enabled him in *The Merchant of Venice* to give the very echo to the place where the Adriatic is enthroned. This is why I believe in representing Portia as a Venetian lady. There are many different ways of playing the part. I have tried five or six ways myself, but I have always come back to the

Italian way, the Renaissance way. In Germany, and allow me here to pay my tribute to Germany—yes I must, although you don't want me to, I can see [1]—for honouring Shakespeare worthily by frequent performances of his plays—in Germany there is a tradition that Portia is a low comedy part. The German Portia is compelled by this tradition (or was when I was last in Germany. Things may have altered) to appear in the Trial Scene in an eighteenth-century wig, horn spectacles, a barrister's cravat, and a fierce moustache. Well, there is something to be said for it. As Sancho Panza remarks, ' an ounce of laughter is better than a pound of care '. Besides, the prodigious wealth of implication in Shakespeare's plays, which makes them all As You Like Its, allows of a great variety of interpretations. But from my point of view, no interpretation entailing a sacrifice of beauty, whether to mirth or to realism, can ever be satisfactory. Portia is the fruit of the Renaissance, the child of a period of beautiful clothes, beautiful cities, beautiful houses, beautiful ideas. She speaks the beautiful language of inspired poetry. Wreck that beauty, and the part goes to pieces.

[1] This parenthesis was interpolated by Ellen Terry during the war. I have preserved it as an interesting record of her independence of mind.

I think Georg Brandes, the Shakespearean commentator I have found of most use to me as an actress, sums up Portia's character as well as it can be done, when he writes that ' in spite of her self-surrender in love there is something independent, almost masculine in her attitude towards life. This orphan heiress has been in a position of authority from childhood. She is used to acting on her own responsibility, without seeking advice first.' It makes me rather impatient when I am told that it is strange that a woman of this type, in the habit of directing herself and directing others, should be willing to be directed by a man so manifestly inferior to her as Bassanio. I think if we take the trouble to enquire into the motives at the back of the famous speech of surrender, it will not strike us as either strange or repellent.

Remember that Portia so far has had everything given to her. She is the spoiled child of fortune, or would be if she were not so generous. It is this excessive generosity which partly explains her offering with herself all she has to the man she loves. We have to take into account too that she is a great lady. ' Noblesse oblige ' was not an empty phrase in her day. Even in our own day a well-bred person who is rich is always anxious not to wound anyone who is poor by even a breath of patronage. When I have added that the first-fruit of love is humility, I need say no more in explanation of Portia's attitude to Bassanio. It seems quite natural that she should assure him that her spirit

> Commits itself to yours to be directed,
> As from her lord, her governor, her king.
> Myself and what is mine to you and yours
> Is now converted : but now I was the lord
> Of this fair mansion, master of my servants,
> Queen o'er myself ; and even now, but now,
> This house, these servants, and this same myself
> Are yours, my lord.

If the speech jars on you—surely such heavenly word-music cannot jar, on the ear at any rate—it is because you take it too literally. I don't mean that Portia is not in earnest. A Cardinal is in earnest when he washes the beggar's feet, but he does not commit himself by this gesture of humility to making a practice of it ! It is clear that Portia's gracious surrender is a ' beau geste ', and little more. The proof is that she retains her independence of thought and action. The first thing she does after her marriage is to lay her own plans for saving Antonio's life, without so much as a ' with your leave or by your leave ' to her lord and master !

The general opinion of Bassanio is unflattering. I

don't know why he is considered such a poor specimen of manhood. My impression is that he has great charm. His loyalty to Antonio is in his favour. He does not let his friend down when he is in trouble. What reason is there to suppose that he will let Portia down, and that she will bitterly regret her marriage? We must not infer that he is stupid because of his failure to recognise Portia in her lawyer's robe at the trial. The impenetrableness of a disguise is a dramatic convention. Shakespeare employs it over and over again.

I have often been asked whether I think Portia's line of pleading in the Court is her own. Was the quibble by which she destroys Shylock's case, and so saves Antonio, her own idea, or did it originate with the learned Bellario? This question interests me more than the one whether the quibble was justified. The answer to this second question is simple. Desperate evils demand desperate remedies. I am driven to think we are dreadfully sentimental nowadays when I hear people say Shylock was infamously treated. He had laid a trap for Antonio, and there was nothing unjust in laying a trap for him. If we regard the Duke's sentence as harsh, especially that clause about Shylock's presently becoming a Christian, we ought to remember that in our own day far more violent animus against the Jewish race has been displayed than in this Venetian Court centuries ago.

But to go back to the question : Who thought of the trap in which Shylock was caught ? It is my belief that it was not a man ! I have an idea that the learned Bellario told Portia at once that the law could not help Antonio. If he turned o'er many books with her (as he says in his letter to the Duke) it was to instruct her in the statutes by which Shylock, in any event, could be punished, not in the hope of proving the bond invalid. He advised her to try an appeal to Shylock's mercy, and if that failed, to try another to his cupidity. If *that* failed, well then I fancy the learned Bellario may have suggested trying a threat. Let the Jew be warned of the consequences of exacting his pound of flesh. To my mind, and I have always tried to show this in the trial scene, Portia is acting on a preconcerted plan up to the moment of pronouncing sentence : then she has an inspiration, and acts on that. Hence her ' Tarry a little ; there is something else '.

There has flashed through her brain suddenly the thought that a pound of flesh is not quite the same thing as a pound of flesh and blood. (We know how careful lawyers have to be when drawing up legal documents, to specify *exactly* what is meant. That is why they are so terribly long.) She tries to disguise her apprehension that this may be a distinction without a difference, and says firmly :

This bond doth give thee here no jot of blood.

I am convinced that this bit of casuistry was not conceived by Shakespeare as being carefully planned. It strikes me as a lightning-like inspiration—just such an inspiration as a woman might have when she is at her wit's end, and is willing to try anything to avoid defeat. Well, whatever view one takes of it, it is impossible to admire it, although it may be defended on the ground that the end justifies the means. From this point in the trial scene the sympathies of a modern audience are with Shylock. Portia's moment is when she appeals to him for mercy.

That famous mercy speech ! To me it will always be a thing ' ensky'd and sainted '. I often pray that to the end of my life I may be able to do *some* justice to these inspired words, written I feel sure to the glory of God, with faith and adoration. The speech is a noble kinsman to the Lord's Prayer, on which indeed it is modelled. It urges with the same beautiful simplicity the same beautiful ideal of justice: ' And forgive us our trespasses as we forgive them that tresspass against us.'

Portia
Then must the Jew be merciful.

Shylock
On what compulsion must I ? tell me that.

Portia
The quality of mercy is not strain'd,
It droppeth as the gentle rain from heaven
Upon the place beneath : it is twice blest ;
It blesseth him that gives and him that takes :
'Tis mightiest in the mightiest ; it becomes
The throned monarch better than his crown ;
His sceptre shows the force of temporal power,
The attribute to awe and majesty,
Wherein doth sit the dread and fear of kings ;
But mercy is above this sceptred sway ;
It is enthroned in the hearts of kings,
It is an attribute to God himself ;
And earthly power doth then show likest God's
When mercy seasons justice. Therefore, Jew,
Though justice be thy plea, consider this,
That, in the course of justice, none of us
Should see salvation : we do pray for mercy ;
And that same prayer doth teach us all to render
The deeds of mercy.

I have done. I want you to go away with those
words in your ears, and to try and make them a living
force in your hearts.

THE PATHETIC WOMEN

THE PATHETIC WOMEN

In my lecture on those women in Shakespeare's plays
I classified as ' triumphant '—and although the label
has been criticised, none of my critics have supplied me
with a better one—I said there was good reason for
believing they were *tall*—strong physically as well as
mentally. I cannot produce any evidence that the
women I am going to talk about in this lecture were
small and slim, of rather frail physique, but that is how
I see them with my mind's eye. Viola in the male
attire she assumes after she has been shipwrecked on the
coast of Illyria looks a slip of a lad. Ophelia, naturally slight, becomes like a wraith of a woman when
her wits go astray. Othello towers over his fragile
Desdemona. I don't conceive Lady Macbeth as a
robust muscular woman, but as a delicate little creature, with hyper-sensitive nerves. This may be the
explanation of my calling these heroines ' pathetic '.
Little creatures *are* pathetic, I think, whether birds,
kittens, or children.

Viola, says her brother Sebastian when he believes her dead, ' bore a mind that envy could not but call fair '. It is a lovely, rather than a brilliant mind. Viola is less witty than either Rosalind or Beatrice. She seldom says a clever thing. She often says a beautiful thing. Shakespeare has put into her mouth some of the most exquisite word-music he ever wrote. Of her it may be said that ' her tongue's sweet air's more tunable than lark to shepherd's ear '. This was the Viola that Ada Rehan brought on to the stage. I shall never forget the beautiful tone of her voice in Viola's reply to the Duke's question : ' How dost thou like this tune ? '

> ' It gives a very echo to the seat
> Where love is throned.'

The Duke's exclamation : ' Thou dost speak masterly ! ' seemed very much to the point. And oh, what wonderful things Ada did with her voice in this speech :

> Make me a willow cabin at your gate,
> And call upon my soul within the house ;
> Write loyal cantons of contemned love,
> And sing them loud even in the dead of night ;
> Halloo your name to the reverberate hills,
> And make the babbling gossip of the air

Cry out ' Olivia ! ' O, you should not rest
Between the elements of air and earth,
But you should pity me !

Then, if ever, we heard the true Shakespearean
music, and I for one was so completely enchanted by
it that I could not agree that Ada Rehan's Viola was
too sophisticated. Years later when I saw my niece
Phyllis in the part I realised however that she, with her
extreme youth, and a heaven-born instinct for acting,
had been able to supply something that was lacking
in Ada Rehan's Viola. Phyllis was but seventeen
years old, and had been on the stage hardly a year
when she gave this exquisite preformance.

Viola has a golden heart as well as a golden voice.
She listens with the most tender sympathy and patience
to Duke Orsino's rhapsodies about Olivia. Imagine
Rosalind or Beatrice in Viola's situation ! Could
either of them have resisted a jest at the unfortunate
Orsino's mad passion ? When Rosalind's Orlando
tells her that neither rhyme nor reason can express how
much he is in love, she smiles and chaffs him :

Love is merely a madness, and I tell you deserves
as well a dark house and a whip as madmen do :
and the reason why they are not so punished and
cured is that the lunacy is so ordinary that the
whippers are in love too.

When Viola's Orsino tells her that he will never accept the situation, never believe that Olivia cannot love him, she speaks to him as tenderly as if he were a sick child clamouring for a toy which must be denied :

> Sooth, but you must.
> Say that some lady, as perhaps there is,
> Hath for your love as great a pang of heart
> As you have for Olivia : you cannot love her ;
> You tell her so : must she not then be answered ?

An honourable, unselfish girl, this Viola. She does not shrink from the very painful task imposed on her of pleading for Orsino to Olivia. And into this vicarious courtship she puts all the passion of love she feels for Orsino :

> If I did love you in my master's flame,
> With such a suffering, such a deadly life,
> In your denial I would find no sense.
> I would not understand it.

Viola, I take it, is very young. Her character seems undeveloped when we compare it with Beatrice's. That may be the explanation of the fact that the part has often been played well by very young actresses. As I have already told you, my niece, Phyllis Neilson-Terry, played it beautifully at the age of seventeen.

The part of Desdemona gives an actress far more difficult problems to solve. I know no character in

Shakespeare which has suffered from so much mis-conception. The general idea seems to be that Des-demona is a ninny, a pathetic figure chiefly because she is half-baked. It is certainly the idea of those who think an actress of the dolly type, a pretty young thing with a vapid innocent expression, is well suited to the part. I shall perhaps surprise you by telling you that a great tragic actress, with a strong personality and a strong method, is far better suited to it, for Desdemona is strong, not weak.

There is something of the potential nun in her. She is more fitted to be the bride of Christ than the bride of any man. Shakespeare implies this in the lines :

> So opposite to marriage that she shunned
> The wealthy curled darlings of our nation.

Her virginal heart is profoundly moved by the meeting with Othello. Unlike the wealthy, curled darlings, this is a man who has suffered many distressful strokes. The story of his life rouses her compassionate interest. As Othello says :

> She lov'd me for the dangers I had pass'd,
> And I lov'd her that she did pity them.

Whereas the handsome faces of the curled darlings had seemed ugly to Desdemona because their minds were ugly, Othello's face seemed fair to her because his mind was fair.

> I saw Othello's visage in his mind,
> And to his honours, and his valiant parts
> Did I my soul and fortunes consecrate.

Desdemona does not use that word 'consecrate' idly. Love to her is a sacrament.

I have said she is a woman of strong character Once she has consecrated herself to Othello, she is capable even of 'downright violence' of all the conventions for his sake. But I think by nature she is unconventional. Othello's doubts that she is chaste are usually made to seem absolutely monstrous in the theatre, because Desdemona's unconventionality is ignored. She is not at all prim or demure ; on the contrary, she is genially expressive, the kind of woman who being devoid of coquetry behaves as she feels. Her manner to Cassio might easily fertilize the poisonous seed of suspicion Iago has sown in Othello's mind. The pertinacity with which she begs Othello to reinstate Cassio does not strike me as evidence that she is a rather foolish woman, lacking in insight. Let an actress give a charming ' I'm really not asking much of you ' tone to Desdemona's suit to her husband, and a very different impression will be produced. Her purity of heart and her charity (charity ' thinketh no evil ') are sufficient explanation of her being slow to grasp the situation. It is not until she has been grossly insulted and brutally assaulted that she understands. Her behaviour from that dreadful moment should surely convince us that she is not a simpleton, but a saint.

There is no scene in the tragedy which throws more light on Desdemona's character than the one in the fourth act between Desdemona and Emilia. Let us study it together. It takes place in Desdemona's room. Othello has just roughly ordered his wife to go to bed, and Emilia is helping her to undress.

Emilia's life has made her cynical about virtue. No wonder ! For one thing, Iago is her husband ! She would not be surprised at frailty in any woman, even in Desdemona. And after all, is this frailty anything to make a fuss about ? There is a curious anticipation of modern ideas in Emilia's attitude.

Desdemona

Dost thou in conscience think—tell me, Emilia,—
That there be women do abuse their husbands
In such gross kind ?

Emilia

There be some such, no question.

Desdemona

Wouldst thou do such a deed for all the world ?

Emilia
  Why, would not you ?

Desdemona
                              No, by this heavenly light !
Emilia
  Nor I neither by this heavenly light.
  I might do't as well i' the dark.

Desdemona
  Wouldst thou do such a deed for all the world ?

Emilia
  The world's a huge thing.   It is a great price
  For a small vice.

Desdemona
  In troth, I think thou wouldst not.

Emilia
  In troth, I think I should—and undo't when I had
    done. . . .

Desdemona
  Beshrew me if I would do such a wrong
  For the whole world. . . .
  I do not think there is any such woman.

Emilia
  Yes, a dozen. . . .
  But I do think it is their husbands' faults
  If wives do fall : say that they slack their duties,
  And pour out treasures into foreign laps,

Or else break out in peevish jealousies,
Throwing restraint upon us ; or say they strike us :
Or scant our former having in despite ;
Why, we have galls, and though we have some
    grace,
Yet have we some revenge.   Let husbands know
Their wives have sense like them : they see and
    smell,
And have their palates both for sweet and sour
As husbands have.   What is it that they do
When they change us for others ? Is it sport ?
I think it is : and doth affection breed it ?
I think it doth : is't frailty that thus errs ?
It is so too.   And have not we affections,
Desires for sport, and frailty, as men have ?
Then let them use us well : else let them know
The ills we do, their ills instruct us so.

Desdemona
Good-night, good-night : heaven me such uses send,
Not to pick bad from bad, but by bad mend.

She has listened patiently. . . .   Yes, there may be
such women . . . but there are others who, like her,
could never pick ' bad from bad '.   Emilia in her heart
knows this.   There will be no reprisals from Desdemona.   Her love for Othello is not of the sort which
' alters when it alteration finds '.

' O, who hath done this deed ? ' cries the distraught
Emilia a few hours later when she finds Desdemona

near to death, and the innocent victim of Iago's devilish plot, with a supreme effort of the love which does not seek its own, whispers faintly the chivalrous falsehood :

> Nobody ; I myself. Farewell :
> Commend me to my kind lord.

Yes, it may be true. Desdemona may have taken her own life. Emilia is pondering this, I think, as she holds her dear mistress in her arms, and then seeing she is dead, lays her back on the disordered bed. She hears Othello's voice saying, ' Why, how should she be murdered ? ' and although she answers ' Alas, who knows ? ' I think she means : ' *You* know ! ' She is beginning to blaze. ' You heard her say herself it was not I.' ' She *said* so ', oh yes ! And Emilia moves away from the deathbed, with the enigmatic remark : ' I must needs report the truth.' Othello seizes her by the arm :

> She's, like a liar, gone to burning hell !
> 'Twas I that killed her.

Emilia has plenty of courage. She is alone with a murderer, a crazy murderer. It is to this that jealousy has brought the noble Moor. She must know that she risks her life by angering him, but she does not care. The slur on the dead woman makes her reckless.

                O the more angel she
And you the blacker devil !

But I must not spoil this wonderful scene by quoting snippets from it.   Listen to it, and see Emilia in an ecstasy of rage, a human volcano in eruption, pouring out a lava of abuse :

Othello
  She turn'd to folly, and she was a whore.

Emilia
  Thou dost belie her, and thou art a devil.

Othello
  She was false as water.

Emilia
              Thou art rash as fire to say
  That she was false : O, she was heavenly true !

Othello
  Cassio did top her : ask thy husband else.
  O, I were damn'd beneath all depth in hell
  But that I did proceed upon just grounds
  To this extremity.   Thy husband knew it all.

Emilia
  My husband !

Othello
  Thy husband.

Emilia
That she was false to wedlock ?

Othello
Ay, with Cassio.   Nay, had she been true,
If heaven would make me such another world
Of one entire and perfect chrysolite,
I 'd not have sold her for it.

Emilia
My husband !

Othello
Ay, 'twas he that told me first :
An honest man he is, and hates the slime
That sticks on filthy deeds.

Emilia
My husband !

Othello
What needs this iteration, woman ? I say, thy husband.

Emilia
My husband say that she was false !

Othello
He, woman ;
I say thy husband ; dost understand the word ?
My friend, thy husband, honest, honest Iago.

Emilia
If he say so, may his pernicious soul
Rot half a grain a day !   He lies to the heart :

She was too fond of her most filthy bargain.
Do thy worst :
This deed of thine is no more worthy heaven
Than thou wast worthy her.

Othello

Peace, you were best !

Emilia
Thou hast not half that power to do me harm
As I have to be hurt. O gull ! O dolt !
As ignorant as dirt ! thou hast done a deed—
I care not for thy sword ;—I'll make thee
    known,
Though I lost twenty lives !

She knows no fear. How she shames the fearful,
those who fear the opinion of the world, or fear to
make themselves ridiculous, or fear the consequences,
and so are silent in the defence of truth.

I, peace !
No ! I will speak as liberal as the north ;
Let heaven, and men, and devils, let them all,
All, all, cry shame against me, yet I'll speak.

It is significant that the chivalrous champions of the
honour of the living Hero, as of the dead Desdemona,
should both be women ! Significant, and original.
Shakespeare is one of the very few dramatists who

seem to have observed that women have more moral courage than men.

He endows Juliet, a very young girl, with the inward freedom which produces this courage. I said just now when I introduced Desdemona that she has been the victim of a great deal of misconception, and I think this is true of Juliet too. Her age may be one of the reasons for this. To us now a girl of fourteen seems a mere child. There is any amount of evidence that in days when the average span of human life was shorter people arrived at maturity sooner. At fourteen, they were not children but adults, and Juliet, at what fourteen meant to Shakespeare, is older than her years. There is some truth in the saying that an actress cannot play Juliet until she is too old to look like Juliet. Whatever her age let her remember that Juliet is something more than a great lover. She is a great poet.

'Truly when I heard Romeo saying : " Ah, she doth teach the torches to burn bright ! " truly my whole being kindled ; I became a flame.'

The actress, to whom those words are attributed by D'Annunzio, had a vein of poetry in her which must have helped her to understand Juliet.

From the first the joy of this passionate young Italian (Shakespeare derived this legend of love and death from Italy and did not attempt to anglicize it)

in finding her mate is overcast by a presentiment of
sorrow :

> My only love sprung from my only hate.
> Too early seen unknown, and known too late.

This ' love eternal in a moment born ' in a Capulet
for a Montague is doomed from birth. It is the con-
viction of this which explains the swiftness of Juliet's
surrender, the boldness of her subsequent actions.
Her courage fails her only once in the play.

She is fearless when she confesses her love :

> My bounty is as boundless as the sea ;
> My love as deep : the more I give to thee
> The more I have, for both are infinite.

She is fearless when she marries her Romeo sec-
retly. She is fearless when he is banished and she has
to face dangers and difficulties alone. . . . During the
brief time between her marriage and her death, her
situation is indeed terrible, but it does not break her
spirit. There is one moment when, driven to desperation, she thinks of putting an end to her life, but like
Joan of Arc, she recants her recantation.

When she parts from Romeo she cannot conceal
her sense of their impending doom :

Juliet
> O think'st thou we shall ever meet again ?

Romeo
I doubt it not ; and all these woes shall serve
For sweet discourses in our time to come.

Juliet
O God, I have an ill-divining soul !
Methinks I see thee, now thou art below,
As one dead in the bottom of a tomb ;
Either my eyesight fails, or thou look'st pale.

Yet that dreadful vision does not appal her, nor
weaken her resistance to her worldly parents. . . .
She fights their plan to marry her to Paris, first with
courage, and when courage is useless and she is over-
come by ' force majeure ', with cunning. Shakespeare gives a terrible picture of parental tyranny in the
scene I am going to read to you :

' Why, how now, Juliet ? ' says her mother, irritated
at the sadness of which she does not know the cause.

Juliet
Madam, I am not well.

Lady Capulet
Evermore weeping for your cousin's death ?
What, wilt thou wash him from his grave with
    tears ? (*You silly child*).
. . . But now I'll tell thee joyful tidings, girl !

Juliet (*rather ironically, I think*)
And joy comes well in such a needy time :
What are they, I beseech your ladyship. . . .

Lady Capulet
　　Marry, my child, early next Thursday morn
　　The gallant, young, and noble gentleman
　　The County Paris, at Saint Peter's Church
　　Shall happily make thee there a joyful bride.

Juliet (horrified)
　　Now by Saint Peter's Church and Peter, too,
　　He shall not make me there a joyful bride.
　　I wonder at this haste ; that I must wed
　　Ere he, that should be husband, comes to woo . . .
　　(Resolutely, though she cannot restrain her tears)
　　I pray you tell my lord and father, madam,
　　I will not marry yet.

Lady Capulet
　　Here comes your father : tell him so yourself
　　And see how he will take it at your hands.
　　　　　　　　　　　　　　(Enter Capulet.)

Capulet
　　How now ! A conduit, girl ? What, still in tears ?
　　Evermore showering ? . . .
　　　　　　　　　　　　How now, wife ?
　　Have you deliver'd to her our decree ?

Lady Capulet
　　Ay, sir, but she will none, she gives you thanks.
　　I would the fool were married to her grave.

Capulet
　　Soft ! take me with you, take me with you, wife.
　　How ? will she none ? doth she not give us thanks ?

141

Is she not proud ? doth she not count her blest,
Unworthy as she is, that we have wrought
So worthy a gentleman to be her bridegroom ?

Juliet

Not proud, you have ; but thankful, that you have :
Proud can I never be of what I hate :
But thankful even for hate, that is meant love.

Capulet

How now, how now, chop-logic ! What is this ?
' Proud '; and ' I thank you '; and ' I thank you not '.
Thank me no thankings, nor proud me no prouds,
But fettle your fine joints 'gainst Thursday next,
To go with Paris to Saint Peter's Church,
Or I will drag thee on a hurdle thither.

Juliet

Good father, I beseech you on my knees
Hear me with patience but to speak a word.

Capulet

Hang thee, young baggage ! disobedient wretch !
I tell thee what : get thee to church o' Thursday
Or never after look me in the face :
Speak not, reply not, do not answer me.

This is too much for Juliet's nurse, old time-server as
she is. Besides, she is cognizant of the situation. She
alone in the Capulet household knows that Juliet is
married to Romeo.

Nurse
>   God in heaven bless her !
> You are to blame, my lord, to rate her so.

Capulet
> And why, my lady wisdom ? hold your tongue.
> Good prudence ; smatter with your gossips, go.

Nurse
> I speak no treason.   May not one speak ?

Capulet
> Peace, you mumbling fool !
> Utter your gravity o'er a gossip's bowl,
> For here we need it not.

Then after a long diatribe on the subject of ungrateful daughters, Capulet delivers his ultimatum.

> Thursday is near ; lay hand on heart, advise :
> An you be mine, I'll give you to my friend.
> An you be not, hang, beg, starve, die in the streets,
> For by my soul I'll ne'er acknowledge thee.

He goes away. That is his last word. In her extremity Juliet appeals to her mother and her nurse for help. Both women have been shocked at Capulet's violence, and have tried to calm him down, but they have no notion of supporting Juliet against him.

Juliet
> Is there no pity sitting in the clouds,
> That sees into the bottom of my grief ?

O, sweet my mother, cast me not away !
Delay this marriage for a month, a week ;
Or, if you do not, make the bridal bed
In that dim monument where Tybalt lies.

Lady Capulet
Talk not to me, for I'll not speak a word :
Do as thou wilt, for I have done with thee.

And she goes away. That is her last word. Poor
Juliet gives a despairing cry ' O God ! ' as her mother
leaves the room. But she is not cowed. There is
plenty of fight in her yet, and she thinks she has a
faithful ally in her nurse!

Juliet
O nurse ! how shall this be prevented ?
. . . . .
What say'st thou ? hast thou not a word of joy ?
Some comfort, nurse.

But all the comfort this depraved old party has to give
is that there is nothing for Juliet to do but make the
best of a bad business, which she insinuates is not so
bad after all.

Nurse
Faith, here it is :
Romeo is banish'd ; and all the world to nothing,
That he dares ne'er come back to challenge you ;
Or if he do, it needs must be by stealth.

Then, since the case so stands as now it doth,
I think it best you married with the county.
O, he's a lovely gentleman. . . .
Romeo's a dishclout to him ! . . .
                       Beshrew my very heart,
I think you are happy in this second match,
For it excels your first ; or if it did not,
Your first is dead ; or 'twere as good he were,
As living here and you no use of him.

Juliet is accustomed to her old nurse's vulgar jokes,
but this one makes her indignant.   Her eyes blaze.

Juliet
  Speakest thou from thy heart ?

Nurse
                       And from my soul too ;
  Or else beshrew them both.

Juliet (*sternly*)
  Amen !

Nurse (*puzzled and rather frightened at the girl's
    manner*)
  What ?

Juliet (*drawing her Italian weapon of dissimulation*)
  Well, thou hast comforted me marvellous much.
  Go in ; and tell my lady I am gone,
  Having displeased my father, to Laurence' cell,
  To make confession, and to be absolved.

Nurse (relieved)
    Marry, I will.   And this is wisely done.

And she ambles out of the room, unconscious that she has appalled her nursling. But *we* know ! Juliet, left alone, denounces her in these magnificent words :

Ancient damnation ! O most wicked fiend !
Is it more sin to wish me thus forsworn,
Or to dispraise my lord with that same tongue
Which she hath praised him with above compare
So many thousand times ? Go, counsellor ;
Thou and my bosom henceforth shall be twain.
I'll to the Friar, to know his remedy :
If all else fail, myself have power to die.

The Friar does not fail Juliet, but he demands a great deal of her. The success of the remedy he suggests depends on her courage and cunning. She is to go home, and pretend to give her consent to the marriage with Paris. The night before the wedding she is to take a potion which will make her unconscious.

No warmth, no breath, shall testify thou livest.

The Friar guarantees that this state will last for forty-two hours, and that everyone will be deceived, and think she is dead. Her body will be taken to the ancient family vault of the Capulets. ' There shall

Romeo come ', and ' he and I will watch thy waking ',
Friar Laurence assures Juliet . . . She might well shrink
from the ordeal, but she does not. She holds out
eager hands for the vial, containing the potion :

> Give me, give me ! O, tell not me of fear !

The change in her is noticed by the Nurse directly
she comes home : ' See where she comes from shrift
with merry look ! ' she says to Capulet. He is in a
better humour than when we saw him last. The pre-
parations for Juliet's wedding to Paris are going
smoothly. All the invitations have been sent out,
extra cooks have been hired, and so on. The silly
child has no doubt been brought to her senses by Friar
Laurence, and he won't have any more trouble with
her. So he greets Juliet quite affectionately :

> How now, my headstrong ! Where have you been
> gadding ?

She, mindful of Friar Laurence's instructions,
assumes a very humble and docile manner, and asks
forgiveness for her disobedience. She uses the weapon
of duplicity very cleverly. Her parents are defeated
by it, completely taken in. The father congratulates
her on her change of heart, says what a wonderful man
the holy friar is (he is indeed !) and goes to the County
Paris to tell him all is well.

In the next scene of the play Juliet is in her bedroom with the Nurse, still acting a part. O that the nurse would go ! It is all that Juliet can do to hide her impatience, as the old woman plagues her to decide what she is going to wear at the wedding. (*Anything will do !*)

> Ay, those attires are best : but, gentle nurse,
> I pray thee, leave me to myself tonight,
> For I have need of many orisons.

Then her lady mother fusses in. Can she help ? ('*I have a lot to do, of course, but still if you want me*'—'*I want you to go ; I want to be alone.*')

Lady Capulet
> What, are you busy, ho ? need you my help ?

Juliet
> No, madam ; we have cull'd such necessaries
> As are behoveful for our state tomorrow :
> So please you, let me now be left alone.

Poor dear ! She's looking very tired. (*And very strange, Lady Capulet, I wonder you don't notice it !*) She ought to go to bed at once and rest. So mother and nurse bid her good-night, and leave the room.

Juliet is alone now, alone with her purpose, alone with her terror. Yes ! For one brief moment she *is* terrified ! The old familiar faces are still dear to her in

spite of everything. . . . Perhaps she will never look
on them again. She is used to having her nurse within
call at night. Many a time that dear nannie has
soothed her when she has been restless, and comforted
her when she woke shuddering from some bad dream.
She is shuddering now, and the impulse to cry out for
help is so overpowering that she can't resist it. But
hardly has she yielded and called 'Nurse!' than she
remembers that she could do nothing for her. She
must face this terror alone :

Farewell ! God knows when we shall meet again.
I have a faint cold fear thrills through my veins
That almost freezes up the heat of life :
I'll call them back again to comfort me.
Nurse ! What should she do here ?
My dismal scene I needs must act alone.
Come, vial !
What if this mixture do not work at all ?
Shall I be married then tomorrow morning ?
No, no, this shall forbid it ; lie thou there.
                              (*Laying down her dagger.*)
What if it be a poison, which the Friar
Subtly hath minister'd to have me dead,
Lest in this marriage he should be dishonour'd
Because he married me before to Romeo ?
I fear it is : and yet methinks it should not,
For he hath still been tried a holy man.
I will not entertain so bad a thought.

How if, when I am laid into the tomb,
I wake before the time that Romeo
Come to redeem me ? there's a fearful point !
Shall I not then be stifled in the vault,
To whose foul mouth no healthsome air breathes
    in,
And there die strangled ere my Romeo comes ?
Or, if I live, is it not very like
The horrible conceit of death and night
Together with the terror of the place,—
As in a vault, an ancient receptacle,
Where, for these many hundred years, the bones
Of all my buried ancestors are pack'd :
Where bloody Tybalt, yet but green in earth,
Lies festering in his shroud, where as they say
At some hours in the night spirits resort :—
Alack, alack, is it not like that I,
So early waking, what with loathsome smells,
And shrieks like mandrakes' torn out of the earth,
That living mortals, hearing them, run mad :—
O, if I wake, shall I not be distraught,
Environed with all these hideous fears ?
And madly play with my forefathers' joints,
And pluck the mangled Tybalt from his shroud ?
And in this rage, with some great kinsman's bone,
As with a club, dash out my desperate brains ?
O, look ! methinks I see my cousin's ghost
Seeking out Romeo, that did spit his body
Upon a rapier's point : stay, Tybalt, stay !
Romeo, I come ! This do I drink to thee !

Ah, if that could be done, as it should be done ! An actress must be in a state of grace to make that speech hers ! She must be on the summit of her art where alone complete abandonment to passion is possible !

Juliet, I once read, but where I cannot remember, is the first sign of a change in Shakespeare's ideas about women. This is something to ponder. It seems to be true that up to the period of his first tragedy, his women characters reveal a certain antagonism to the whole sex. Think of Adriana in *The Comedy of Errors*, of Katherine in *The Taming of the Shrew*. They don't inspire us with love or admiration. The hysterical Lady Anne in *Richard III* is frankly a study of feminine weakness. Helena in *All's Well that Ends Well*, and Julia in *Two Gentlemen of Verona* belong to the ' doormat ' type. They bear any amount of humiliation from the men they love, seem almost to enjoy being maltreated and scorned by them, and hunt them down in the most undignified way when they are trying to escape. The fraud with which Helena captures Bertram, who has left his home and country to get away from her, is really despicable. Coleridge must have forgotten Helena when he wrote : ' In Shakespeare all the elements of womanhood are holy.' [1]

---

[1] He had not forgotten her, however. He actually refers to Helena as ' the loveliest of Shakespeare's characters ' !—C. St. J.

What was the cause of the change which drew Shakespeare to the creation of great-hearted, great-minded, lovable women ? There is a theory, and a very plausible one, it seems to me, that when he first came to London and began writing comedies, he was still smarting under the disillusionment of his own unfortunate marriage. The women characters are either like the unamiable shrew that his wife was, or like the patient Griselda that he thought she ought to have been !

Then Mistress Mary Fitton came upon the scene, a fine creature in spite of that fault she had to excess, and the ' powerful might ' of her vivid personality widened and intensified the vision of the man who loved her. . . . I am attracted by this theory, but I have to warn myself and you of the danger of becoming obsessed by any *one* theory about Shakespeare ! The web of life, he tells us, ' is of a mingled yarn ', and this is true of the web of life in his plays. Mary Fitton is only one strand in it. If we believe the legend of his passionate love for Mary Fitton—and why should we not, since there is no smoke without fire ?—we shall think it extremely probable that she was the begetter of many of those touches of aristocratic pride, of brilliant spirits, of witty speech, in his portraits of women. It says much for Shakespeare—and for her too—that in spite of the unfortunate and unhappy outcome of his devotion, he was not embittered. With one notable exception, Cressida, the women in the plays of his maturity afford evidence of this.

What a wonderful study of a mother he gives us in Constance in *King John*. That inordinate love, that inordinate grief, how well we who are mothers can understand both !

There is an equally wonderful study of a daughter in *King Lear*. Perhaps some of you have a daughter, who like Cordelia is extremely reticent, loves you dearly, but never gushes. Perhaps there is a daughter here who knows exactly what Cordelia means when she says her love is ' more richer than her tongue '.

' Made she no verbal question ? ' Kent asks the man who has taken Cordelia the news of the cruelty which has been meted out to her father by her sisters, and he answers :

'Faith, once or twice she heaved the name of 'father'
Pantingly forth, as if it press'd her heart :
Cried ' Sisters ! Sisters ! Shame of ladies ! Sisters !
Kent ! Father ! Sisters ! What, i' the storm ?
    'i the night ?
Let pity not be believed ! ' There she shook
The holy water from her heavenly eyes,
And clamour moisten'd : then away she started
To deal with grief alone.

Burning shame, Kent says in this same scene, keeps Lear from going to Cordelia in his extremity, but when they meet again she makes things beautifully easy for him. It is doubtful whether she even remembers how cruelly he once misunderstood her. She never reproaches him for having disinherited her, and given her dower to her sisters. Her one thought is to make up to him for their brutality and pour balm into his wounds :

> O my dear father ! Restoration hang
> Thy medicine on my lips ; and let this kiss
> Repair those violent harms that my two sisters
> Have in thy reverence made ! . . .
> Had you not been their father, these white flakes
> Had challenged pity of them. Was this a face
> To be opposed against the warring winds ?
> To stand against the deep dread bolted thunder ?
>   . . . Mine enemy's dog,
> Though he had bit me, should have stood that night
> Against my fire ; and wast thou fain, poor father,
> To hovel thee with swine, and rogues forlorn,
> In short and musty straw ? Alack, alack !
> 'Tis wonder that thy life and wits at once
> Had not concluded all. He wakes ; speak to
> him.

We can tell from this how shy she is. She becomes embarrassed directly her father is conscious.

The Doctor
  Madam, do you : 'tis fittest.

Cordelia
  How does my royal lord ? How fares your Majesty ?

Lear
  You do me wrong to take me out o' the grave :
  Thou art a soul in bliss ; but I am bound
  Upon a wheel of fire, that mine own tears
  Do scald like molten lead.

Cordelia
                    Sir, do you know me ?

Lear
  You are a spirit, I know ; when did you die ?

Cordelia
  Still, still, far wide.

Doctor
  He's scarce awake ; let him alone awhile.

Lear
  Where have I been ? Where am I ? Fair daylight ?
  I am mightily abused. I should e'en die with pity,
  To see another thus. I know not what to say.
  I will not swear these are my hands : let's see ;
  I feel this pin prick. Would I were assured
  Of my condition !

Cordelia
              O, look upon me, sir,
  And hold your hands in benediction o'er me :
  No, sir, you must not kneel.

Lear

                           Pray, do not mock me :
I am a very foolish, fond old man,
Fourscore and upward, not an hour more nor less ;
And, to deal plainly,
I fear I am not in my perfect mind.
Methinks I should know you, and know this man ;
Yet I am doubtful : for I am mainly ignorant
What place this is ; and all the skill I have
Remembers not these garments ; nor I know not
Where I did lodge last night. Do not laugh at me :
For, as I am a man, I think this lady
To be my child Cordelia.

Cordelia

                           And so I am, I am.

Lear

Be your tears wet ? yes, 'faith. I pray, weep not :
If you have poison for me, I will drink it.
I know you do not love me ; for your sisters
Have, as I do remember, done me wrong ;
You have some cause, they have not.

Cordelia

                           No cause, no cause.

Kind and dear princess ! Still waters run deep !
That sums up her character. Cordelia is a most difficult part. So little to say, so much to feel ! Rarely
does an actress fathom the depths of those still waters.

A greater contrast to Cordelia than Cleopatra could hardly be conceived. The moral contrast is sufficiently obvious. I am not referring to that, but to the contrast between Cordelia's reticence and Cleopatra's ebullience. I think Cleopatra is the most expressive of all Shakespeare's heroines. She can put all her emotions into words, and she gives me the impression sometimes of saying more than she feels. I believe Shakespeare conceived her as a woman with a shallow nature, and I should like to see her played as such. If she were not idealized in the theatre, it would be clear to us that Shakespeare has done what no other writer, novelist, dramatist or poet has done—told the truth about the wanton. Yes, Cleopatra is that, and if she is represented as a great woman with a great and sincere passion for Antony, the part does not hang together.

It is said that Shakespeare had many collaborators in *Henry VIII*, but I'll be sworn Queen Katharine is all his work. Who but Shakespeare could have shown in a few deft touches how the elements are mixed up in this nature, pride and humility, rebelliousness and resignation, hardness and softness? Katharine is another example of Shakespeare's sensitiveness to racial characteristics. Surely she is as Spanish as Volumnia is Roman and Juliet Italian. It is the punctilious

Spaniard, who sick unto death, rouses herself to rebuke a messenger who has failed in respect :

> You are a saucy fellow :
> Deserve we no more reverence ?

The Queen's faithful old servant Griffith intervenes as the ' saucy fellow ' does not take the hint.

> You are to blame,
> Knowing she will not lose her wonted greatness,
> To use so rude behaviour : go to, kneel.

Shakespeare had something to go on when he created this queen. Her history, and very recent history it was to him, was well known. But the queen of his imagination, Hermione in *The Winter's Tale*, is every bit as grand and gracious a figure. The loyalty Hermione shows to the husband who has slandered her, without abating a jot of her dignity, reminds us of Katharine's to Henry. Hermione has been cruelly and falsely accused. Yet she has more pity for her accuser than for herself. She knows that jealousy has made him for the time insane, and that when he comes to his senses he will suffer agonies of remorse.

> How will this grieve you,
> When you shall come to clearer knowledge, that
> You thus have punished me !

Dignity under a false accusation, unwavering love in spite of it, were evidently greatly admired by Shakespeare, for he exalts them again in Imogen. I am 'foolish fond' of this heroine. When I am asked which is my favourite part, her name rises spontaneously to my lips. She enchants me, and so I can find no fault in her. Well, I am in good company. Two poets, Tennyson and Swinburne, loved Imogen above all Shakespeare's women. Swinburne calls her the 'crown-flower' of his genius. And Bernard Shaw says she is an enchanting person of the most delicate sensitiveness, and of the highest breeding and courage. She needs the highest courage, for she is made to suffer trial after trial. When I came to know her well—it was in 1896, the year *Cymbeline* was produced at the Lyceum—I was able to understand how, after all the crimes her husband Leonatus Posthumus has committed against her—the worst I think is his writing that lying love-letter to bring her to Milford Haven within reach of his revenge—she can throw her arms round him and say in an ecstasy of tenderness :

Why did you throw your wedded lady from you ?
Think that you are upon a rock ; and now
Throw me again.

That is just what a very impulsive person *would* say ! And Imogen is impulsive above all things.

Her impulses are always wholehearted ones too. She never does anything by halves. This is shown very clearly in her scene with Iachimo in the second act. Her indignation with him for traducing her husband and trying to undermine her loyalty is intense, but it passes quickly when Iachimo, seeing he has made a mistake, begins to praise him.

At the words :

> . . . Such a holy witch
> That he enchants societies unto him ;
> Half all men's hearts are his—

she is radiant again, and has forgotten her resentment.

' You make amends ', she says generously. So swift are Imogen's changes of mood that the actress who plays her has hard work to make her a consistent character. Her heart has reasons that reason cannot understand.

It seems strange to me that anyone can think of Lady Macbeth as a sort of monster, abnormally hard, abnormally cruel, or visualize her as a woman of powerful physique, with the muscles of a prize-fighter ! But it is clear from records of some performances of the part, and from portraits of the actresses who gave them, that it can be done ! I have already told you I conceive Lady Macbeth as a small, slight woman of acute nervous sensibility, and now I must try to tell you why. I don't think my conception is contradicted by the lines in which Lady Macbeth reproaches Macbeth for his pusillanimity. As I construe them, they support it.

> I have given suck, and know
> How tender 'tis to love the babe that milks me ;
> I would, while it was smiling in my face,
> Have plucked my nipple from his boneless gums,
> And dashed the brains out, had I so sworn as you
> Have done to this.

Are not these lines capable of *this* construction : ' I would do all that I *couldn't* do, all that would be utterly false to every natural instinct and feeling of mine, rather than break such an oath as the one you have sworn.'

This frenzied appeal is surely the expression of the desperation Lady Macbeth feels at the sudden paralysis of Macbeth's faculties in the hour of action. He must be roused, he must be roused. Is all they have gone through to be for nothing ? She is beside herself. We really ought not to take her wild words as a proof of abnormal ferocity.

She has never failed her husband yet. The relation between them is not that of master and subject. They are on the terms of equals. She has always been fully cognizant of his plans, and helped him to carry them out. Macbeth calls her ' my dearest partner of greatness ', and it is as partners they engage in crime. The wife is compelled to take up the burden of action when the husband, who being a dreamer finds it intolerably heavy, lays it down. Lady Macbeth's nervous force sustains her until Duncan's murder is accomplished. Then she collapses, and faints ! I suppose I can say : ' *That's* womanly ' !

Henceforth she is ' troubled with thick-coming fancies '. In plain prose she has a nervous break-down. She is haunted by the horror of the murder. It preys upon her mind, and saps her physical strength. She dies of remorse. Surely this is good evidence that she is not of the tigress type, mentally or physically.

From all accounts by Mrs. Siddons's contemporaries, there would seem to be no doubt that she played Lady Macbeth on the ' tigress ' lines, creating a woman of inhuman strength (an ' exultant savage ' says one witness), but her memoranda about the part prove that she did not *see* her like that. She thought that Lady Macbeth was ' fair, feminine, nay, perhaps even fragile '. If there was such a difference, as this note indicates, between the great actress's theory and practice, it would not surprise me. I know that I have expressed opinions in these lectures about some of

Shakespeare's women which do not coincide with those I have expressed in my acting. It is not always possible for us players to portray characters on the stage exactly as we see them in imagination. Mrs. Siddons may have realized that her physical appearance alone—her aquiline nose, her raven hair, her flashing eyes, her commanding figure—was against her portraying a fair, feminine, 'nay, perhaps even fragile' Lady Macbeth. It is no use an actress wasting her nervous energy on a battle with her physical attributes. She had much better find a way of employing them as allies.

I once had in my possession a little pencil sketch—oh where is it now, the lost, stolen or borrowed treasure!—of Mrs. Siddons making her exit in the sleep-walking scene. It was given me by that member of her family we used to call 'young Kemble' long after he became old Kemble. He told me it was the work of a contemporary who had seen Mrs. Siddons as Lady Macbeth, so the representation of the exit may be assumed to have some value as a record. It confirms the tradition that it was made in the whirlwind style, a tradition which has led some people to imagine that this was the style in which the actress played the whole scene. I have wondered and wondered about that, and always come to the conclusion that it is improbable, almost impossible, for technical reasons.

A story told me by Henry Irving is something to go on. He had the story from a Mr. A., who was alive until quite recently. Mr. A.'s father frequented a coffee-house in the City. Another regular customer was a very old man, still very handsome, and very deaf.

' That's John Philip Kemble '. The waiters used to point him out with pride to the other customers. ' No one dare speak to him. He loses his temper when he don't hear, and he often don't, because he's deaf.'

However, Mr. A.'s father, a theatre enthusiast, kept on watching for an opportunity for getting into conversation with the old actor, and one day it came when after handing him the mustard, he was rewarded by a genial ' Thank'ee, sir.' This encouraged him to shout—he had to shout it—' I wonder if you could tell me something I want to know about your sister Sarah ? '

The handsome old man frowned. The question had to be repeated several times before he spoke.

' Sarah ? Oh yes—you're quite right. She *was* a fine actress.'

This was baffling, but Mr. A. persisted :

' I want to know what she did in the sleep-walking scene.'

' Sarah cut the sleep-walking scene ? Oh dear no ! She didn't cut a word ! '

'What was her method in the scene?' Mr. A. bellowed.

'*Method?* Sarah's method? Let me think. Sarah's method? Well, let me see—' He rubbed his chin thoughtfully. '*She never moved!*'

I don't know what Mr. A. made of this, but it conveys a great deal to me about Mrs. Siddons's treatment of the scene. The effect of her whirlwind exit must have been tremendous after that immobility.

'But soft! The fair Ophelia! Sweet rose of May!' The whole tragedy of *her* life is that she is afraid; I think I am right in saying she is Shakespeare's only timid heroine. She is scared of Hamlet when trouble changes him from the 'point-devise' lover—the 'glass of fashion and the mould of form'—into a strange moody creature, careless of his appearance, bitter in his speech, scornful of society. She is scared of her father, and dare not disobey him, even when he tells her to play the spy on Hamlet. She is scared of life itself when things go wrong. Her brain, her soul and her body are all pathetically weak. It is not surprising that she should think Hamlet mad, for all he says in the scene in which she returns his presents is completely beyond her. If this scene is rightly acted, we feel a great compassion for the poor girl, whom Hamlet at once loves and hates. I think it ought to be suggested from the first that there is something queer about her, something which explains her wits going astray later on. Her father's murder is assigned as the reason, but it seems more likely that this shock developed an incipient insanity. Ophelia is really mad, not merely metaphorically mad—with grief.

The mad were harshly treated in Shakespeare's day. Ophelia escapes the dark house and the whip, but she is avoided by everyone. The poor demented creature wanders about by the river, in and out of the palace rooms, without a soul to look after her. Her father is dead, her brother is away, the King and Queen shrink from seeing or speaking with her. ' I will not speak with her ', Queen Gertrude says impatiently. ' What would she have ? '

Ophelia makes them feel particularly uncomfortable for reasons implied by Shakespeare in this speech by a gentleman at the court, a very valuable speech to the actress, who can learn from it how the famous ' mad ' scene ought to be played :

She is importunate, indeed distract. . . .
She speaks much of her father, says she hears
There's tricks i' the world ; and hems, and beats
  her heart ;
Spurns enviously at straws ; speaks things in doubt,
That carry but half sense : her speech is nothing,

Yet the unshaped use of it doth move
The hearers to collection ; they aim at it,
And botch the words up fit to their own thoughts ;
Which, as her winks, and nods, and gestures yield
        them,
Indeed would make one think there might be
        thought,
Though nothing sure, yet much unhappily.

When Laertes returns he hardly recognises his sister,
' the fair Ophelia ', ' the rose of May ', in this poor
derelict. ' Had thou thy wits, and didst persuade
revenge ', he cries, ' it could not move thus.' And I
think there is no ' sane ' scene in Shakespeare which
moves us as much as this ' mad ' one, this beautiful
painful scene in which Ophelia prattles and sings,
making one think, as the observant courtier says, ' there
might be thought, though nothing sure.' [1]

'Come, my coach ! Good-night, ladies ! Good-
night, sweet ladies ; good-night, good-night.'

[1] When Ellen Terry delivered this lecture she usually left her
reading-desk at this point, and acted the scene. She judged it impossible to read it. She ended the lecture with Ophelia's last words,
which are printed above.

THE LETTERS IN SHAKESPEARE'S PLAYS

THE LETTERS IN SHAKESPEARE'S PLAYS

THERE have been times during the preparation of these lectures when, thinking of the great mass of literature on the subject of Shakespeare, I have despaired of finding anything to say about him which has not been said before. I recall some lines in one of his sonnets which describe better than I can what I have felt about my task :

> If there be nothing new, but that which is
> Hath been before, how are our brains beguiled,
> That, labouring for invention, bear amiss
> The second burden of a former child.

Nevertheless I have some reason for believing that the subject of this lecture—the letters in Shakespeare's plays—has not been dealt with before. The letters are not as familiar as the songs, which have frequently been published together in many different forms. When I suggested to a scholarly friend that a little volume of the letters, with notes on their writers and readers, would be welcome, I was told that there were too few for such a publication. This induced me to count them for the first time, and perhaps you will be as surprised as my scholarly friend was to hear that they number thirty-four ! And all these thirty-four letters are well worth reading for their intrinsic interest. A letter is a favourite device with dramatists, but few of them do more than make it serve its explanatory purpose. Shakespeare does much more. The letters he wrote for his characters are human documents, one of the many proofs that he was never driven by the exigencies of the theatre to depart from the truth.

They are all the more precious because they are the only letters written by him which have been preserved. Were there many letters from him to his family, his friends, his fellow-actors, his fellow-dramatists, which have perished? I doubt it. It seems unlikely that he was a prolific letter-writer. He crowded his great life's work, which has made England more honoured throughout the world than the achievements of her great soldiers, sailors and statesmen, into a score of years. He did not begin his career as a youthful prodigy and he died when he was fifty-two. What with adapting plays, creating them, retouching them at rehearsal, writing sonnets, acting, managing companies of actors and having a good time with his friends, he could not have had much leisure for pouring out his soul in letters. The man who does that is, as a rule, an idle man, and Shakespeare, I feel sure, was always busy.

People often say we have no authority for talking about Shakespeare as a man at all. What do we know for certain about his life ? Well, I agree with Georg Brandes (my favourite Shakespearean commentator) that, given the possession of forty-five important works by any man, it is entirely our own fault if we know nothing about him. But perhaps these works are not by Shakespeare, but by a syndicate of dramatists, or by some fellow who took his name ! That fellow Bacon, for instance ! The pursuit of these fantastic theories has always seemed to me a waste of time. I wish we had just one authentic letter of Shakespeare's to put a stop to it.

The first letter I am going to read is a love-letter. Love-letters seldom interest anyone except the lover and the beloved. Their contents and their form alike are seldom distinguished by originality. Brilliant people and stupid people use the same vocabulary. Shakespeare is right in making the intellectual Hamlet begin his love-letter to Ophelia in the conventional language of gallantry :

To the celestial and my soul's idol, the most beau-tified Ophelia—In her excellent white bosom—

and so on.

The poem which follows is in the same exaggerated strain :

> Doubt thou the stars are fire,
> > Doubt that the sun doth move,
>
> Doubt truth to be a liar,
> > But never doubt I love.

Then Hamlet, always self-critical, feels the emptiness of these artificial phrases and expresses himself more simply and spontaneously :

> O dear Ophelia, I am ill at these numbers ; I have not art to reckon my groans ; but that I love thee best, O most best, believe it. Adieu.
> Thine evermore, most dear lady, whilst this machine is to him, HAMLET.

Is he sincere ? Does he really love Ophelia ? There has been nearly as much argument about this as about his madness. The truth seems to be that he was deeply, passionately in love with Ophelia, yet was fully conscious of her limitations. The revelation of his mother's frailty then filled him with loathing for this passion of love. He began to see it in its ugliest aspect, stripped of romance, and despised himself for having been swept away by it. His attitude in the scene in which Ophelia returns his presents is evidence of this. Brutality and tenderness are mingled in it. His words are those of a man who loves, and hates the base and impure elements in love. 'I did love you once' 'I love you not', he cries, and both these assertions are true. His struggle to cast Ophelia out of his life is eased by the discovery that she is too weak to stand by him and can be made the tool of his enemies. But he does not forget her. Her tragic death moves him deeply and wrings from him the confession of the truth he may often have denied, in anger at being enslaved by love :

> I loved Ophelia. Forty thousand brothers
> Could not, with all their quantity of love,
> Make up my sum.

'The fair Ophelia.' 'The rose of May.' She was very beautiful, this poor weak-witted girl, and Hamlet was subjugated by her beauty. Who can doubt it ?

In writing those 'numbers', at which Hamlet says in his letter he is ill, Proteus, an expert lover, excels. I can imagine this gentleman of Verona spinning off yards of amorous doggerel without the slightest effort. Of his letter to Julia we hear only the few broken sentences she can decipher from the bits she pieces together after she has repented of having torn it up. 'Kind Julia' : 'Love-wounded Proteus' : 'Poor forlorn Proteus' : 'Passionate Proteus.' But they are instructive. It is clear that there was more about Proteus than about

Julia in that letter ! Well, it is not unusual for lovers
to be more interested in themselves than in their mis-
tresses. Valentine's letter to Silvia is a good illustra-
tion of this. We hear this letter in its entirety.
Valentine plays prettily enough with words ; his
rhymes are neat, but the note of genuine emotion
is never sounded in this jingle :

> My thoughts do harbour with my Silvia nightly,
> And slaves they are to be that send them flying :
> O, could their master come and go as lightly,
> Himself would lodge where senseless they are lying !
> My herald thoughts in thy pure bosom rest them,
> While I, their king, that thither them importune,
> Do curse the grace that with such grace hath blest
> them,
> Because myself do want my servants' fortune.
> I curse myself, for they are sent by me,
> That they should harbour where their lord should be.

What a contrast between the ' love ' expressed in this
letter, a mere selfish desire for the gratification of the
senses, and the love which does not seek its own,
expressed in the wonderful letter from Antonio to
Bassanio ! Of all the letters in the plays this is the one
which moves me most.

> Sweet Bassanio, my ships have all miscarried, my
> creditors grow cruel, my estate is very low, my bond
> to the Jew is forfeit ; and since in paying it, it is

impossible I should live, all debts are cleared between you and I, if I might but see you at my death. Notwithstanding, use your pleasure ; if your love do not persuade you to come, let not my letter.

Antonio's love has all the tenderness of a woman's : (' Sweet Bassanio ' !) : the trustfulness of a child's : (I have only to tell him of my plight and he will help me) ; the generosity and manliness of a true friend : (Don't feel that you owe me anything. It's all right, but I would like to see you once more and grasp your hand) ; the unselfishness of a devoted wife's, or a devoted mother's : (You mustn't think of coming all the same, if it puts you out). Truly a divine letter !

Our manner of expression is determined by the age in which we live, but in this letter it is the thing expressed that seems to have changed. It is impossible to study Shakespeare's plays closely without noticing that to him friendship was perhaps the most sacred of all human relations. Valentine offers to sacrifice Silvia to Proteus. Bassanio says that his wife matters less to him than the life of his friend. To an Elizabethan audience this exaltation of friendship did not seem strange. Two of Shakespeare's comrades, Beaumont and Fletcher, lived together ' on the Bankside, not far from the playhouse ', and had the same ' clothes and cloak between them ' ; and there were many such all-sufficing friendships. That attractive old sinner, John Falstaff, was cut to the heart when his friend Prince Hal publicly denounced him. His affection for young Harry is a lovable trait in his character ; and who does not feel sorry for him, worthless old waster as he is, when the Prince answers his salutation : ' God save thee, my sweet boy ', with the freezing rebuke : ' I know thee not, old man ; fall to thy prayers ' ? But when Falstaff wrote the following letter, Prince Hal had not finished sowing his wild oats, and was still on intimate terms with the ' old man '. He had, however, as the letter shows, begun to show a preference for the company of Poins, which makes Falstaff fear his influence is on the wane. It is Poins who reads the letter to the Prince, and we may be sure he gives the references to himself an ironical emphasis :

Sir John Falstaff, knight, to the son of the King, nearest his father, Harry Prince of Wales, greeting :
I will imitate the honourable Romans in brevity. . . . I commend me to thee, I commend thee, and I leave thee. Be not too familiar with Poins ; for he misuses thy favours so much, that he swears thou art to marry his sister Nell. Repent at idle times as thou mayest, and so, farewell.
Thine by yea and no, which is as much as to say, as thou usest him, Jack Falstaff with my familiars,

John with my brothers and sisters and Sir John with all Europe.

The effect of the letter on the Prince is not to make him distrust Poins, but to inspire him to pay Falstaff out for presuming to criticise his friend. 'How might we see Falstaff bestow himself to-night in his true colours and not ourselves be seen ?' Poins suggests that they should put on two leathern jerkins, and wait upon the fat knight, who is supping with Mistress Doll Tearsheet at the Boar's Head, at table as drawers. This prank (the last Prince Hal plays on Falstaff, for soon after his visit to the Boar's Head, he mends his madcap ways and becomes dignified, sober and virtuous) is the theme of one of the most broadly comic scenes in the second part of *Henry IV*. Falstaff pretends not to recognise the drawers, but I think the Prince is right in his surmise that he knew who was at his back, and revelled in the opportunity for scoring off them. The spectator of this scene should, if the actor who plays Falstaff sets off his wit with charm, be able to say as sincerely as Doll Tearsheet : 'I love thee better than I love e'er a scurvy young boy of them all.'

When we meet Falstaff again in *The Merry Wives of Windsor*—in which play Shakespeare had to bring him out of his grave, 'by request', because he was so popular in the theatre that audiences wanted to see him in

another play—we still love him, but we have to admit
he has deteriorated. His wit is not so brilliant. He
has become more garrulous, in his letters as well as in
his conversation. You may remember that he writes
two love-letters, word for word the same, to two
women living in the same town, who, as he must have
known, met often and exchanged confidences. This
alone shows that the Falstaff of the *Merry Wives* is not
quite the man he was in *Henry IV*. Perhaps this is
because he does not carry his sack quite as well !
Still there are some delightfully Falstaffian touches in
the letter Mrs. Page reads, chuckling at having ''scaped
love-letters in the holiday-time of her beauty', and
now being ' a subject for them ' :

> Ask me no reason why I love you ; for though Love
> use Reason for his physician, he admits him not for
> his counsellor. You are not young, no more am I ;
> go to, then, there's sympathy : you are merry, so am
> I ; ha, ha ! then there's more sympathy : you
> love sack, and so do I ; would you desire better sym-
> pathy ? Let it suffice thee, Mistress Page,—at the
> least, if the love of soldier can suffice,—that I love
> thee. I will not say, pity me ; 'tis not a soldier-like
> phrase ; but I say, love me. By me,
>
> > Thine own true knight,
> > By day or night,
> > Or any kind of light,

> With all his might
> For thee to fight,
>
> JOHN FALSTAFF.

This letter tickles us as much to-day—that is when it is read aloud, for in print it is not very funny—as it tickled Shakespeare's contemporaries over three centuries ago. Wonderful, for humour is the element in drama most affected by time. Remove a joke from its place in time, and it ceases to exist as a joke. The human sense of what is tragic has changed very little ; but the human sense of what is comic changes almost as rapidly as fashions in dress. So comedies soon begin to ' date '. It may be because Shakespeare saw and used the fun of the relatively durable things in life, that it has not become obsolete. His comedy is not always ' quite nice ', but it is quite mirth-provoking, that is, if it is not treated academically. If a modern audience does not laugh at Shakespeare's jokes, blame the actors !

The letter that Maria, in *Twelfth Night*, palms off on Malvolio as Olivia's has all the material for making us laugh ; but I have seen the material used on the stage in a way which justified the sad solemnity of the audience. Given good comedians, the situation in which Maria's letter is read will always be good fun. It begins in verse—the fashionable medium for a love-letter in Shakespeare's time—and it must have been difficult for Shakespeare to write such bad verse as this !

> Jove knows I love ;
>> But who ?
> Lips, do not move ;
> No man must know.
> I may command where I adore ;
>> But silence, like a Lucrece knife,
> With bloodless stroke my heart doth gore :
>> M, O, A, I, doth sway my life !

Maria is not much of a poet, but when she takes to prose, she shines !

If this fall into thy hand, revolve. In my stars I am above thee, but be not afraid of greatness. Some are born great, some achieve greatness and some have greatness thrust upon 'em. Thy Fates open their hands ; let thy blood and spirit embrace them ; and, to inure thyself to what thou art like to be, cast thy humble slough and appear fresh. Be opposite with a kinsman, surly with servants ; let thy tongue tang arguments of state ; put thyself into the trick of singularity : she thus advises thee that sighs for thee. Remember who commended thy yellow stockings and wished to see thee ever cross-gartered. I say, remember. Go to, thou art made, if thou desirest to be so ; if not, let me see thee a steward still, the fellow of servants and not worthy to touch

Fortune's fingers. Farewell. She that would alter services with thee,

THE FORTUNATE-UNHAPPY.

Then follows the postscript; and Maria had reserved her great coup for the postscript:

Thou canst not choose but know who I am. If thou entertainest my love, let it appear in thy smiling. Thy smiles become thee well; therefore in my presence still smile, dear my sweet, I prithee!

Shakespeare was no Puritan. He probably enjoyed bear-baiting, and yet, unlike many of his contemporaries, felt sorry for the bear. So after writing this scene, in which Malvolio is baited and deluded and made to look a fool, he is able to write another in which our sympathies are roused with the victim of Maria's 'sport royal'. Malvolio's letter to Olivia makes us see the sport in its cruel aspect.

By the Lord, Madam, you wrong me, and the world shall know it. Though you have put me into darkness and given your drunken cousin rule over me, yet have I the benefit of my senses as well as your ladyship. I have your own letter that induced me to the semblance I put on; with the which I doubt not but to do myself much right, or you much shame. Think of me as you please. I leave my duty a little unthought of and speak out of my injury.

THE MADLY-USED MALVOLIO.

183

Although written in circumstances calculated to make the best servant ' a little ' forget his duty, this letter is full of the dignity of service, and a just rebuke to those who hold their ' inferiors ' up to ridicule.

From a letter from a steward in a gold chain, preserving his dignity in an undignified position, I turn to one from a groom. A plain fellow this. I see him sitting down, laboriously scratching out a few illegible sentences. But they are straight to the point, and they have their dramatic value in adding a vivid touch to the portrait of Cardinal Wolsey in *Henry VIII*.

MY LORD,—The horses your lordship sent for, with all the care I had, I saw well chosen, ridden, and furnished. They were young and handsome, and of the best breed in the north. When they were ready to set out for London, a man of my Lord Cardinal's, by commission and main power, took 'em from me, with this reason : His master would be served before a subject, if not before the King ; which stopped our mouths, sir.

There is a tedious letter in *Love's Labour's Lost*, which must have amused Shakespeare's contemporaries because it satirizes the affectations of their day. Armado's style in this letter is only a slight exaggeration of that in which people wrote to Queen Elizabeth. They used six long words when one short one would have conveyed

their meaning, and racked their brains for pretentious
and extravagant compliments. Here is a sample of
Armado's euphuism. It is written to Jacquenetta, a
country girl, who has attracted the magnificent
Spaniard,

> A man in all the world's new fashion planted,
> That hath a mint of phrases in his brain.

The magnanimous and most illustrate king Cophetua
set eye upon the pernicious and indubitate beggar,
Zenelophon ; and he it was that might rightly say,
Veni, vidi, vici ; which to annothanize in the vulgar,
—O base and obscure vulgar !—videlicet, He came,
saw, and overcame : he came, one ; saw, two ;
overcame, three. Who came ? The king. Why
did he come ? To see. Why did he see ? To over-
come. To whom came he ? To the beggar. What
saw he? The beggar. Who overcame he? The beggar. The conclusion is victory; on whose side? The
king's. The captive is enriched ; on whose side ?
The beggar's. The catastrophe is a nuptial; on whose
side? The king's; no, on both in one, or one in both.

And so forth !

Of course the drollness of the letter lies chiefly in its
having been written by the magnificent Armado to a
stolid illiterate peasant girl. In the theatre we have
seen them both and can appreciate the absurdity of this,
especially if Boyet, who has to read Armado's pedantic

circumlocutions, is a good actor. But if he is a wise one he will beg leave to cut some of them, as I confess I have done !

There is another letter from Armado to the King which is an even choicer specimen of Elizabethan jargon. Did I hear a groan ? It's all right ! I am not going to read it ! I am going to stop at telling you that it is a lesson to us all to let our yea be yea and our nay nay. Armado's never are. He scorns to tell the King that he went for a walk in the evening at six. He must write that he ' betook himself to walk ', that the time was ' about the sixth hour when beasts most graze, birds best pick, and men sit down to *that nourishment called supper* ' ! Well, there are plenty of modern Armados. Jargon is still talked and written. Don't they say in the House of Commons that ' the answer to the question is in the negative ' ? That strikes me as a very Armado-like circumlocution for ' No '.

' I say she never did invent this letter ', exclaims Rosalind, after her first glance at the rhymed jingle that Phebe sends her under the impression that she is a handsome young man. Rosalind accuses Phebe's shepherd lover, Silvius, of its authorship, but he swears Phebe wrote it :

> I know not the contents : but as I guess
> By the stern brow and waspish action

Which she did use as she was writing of it,
It bears an angry tenour.

Shepherds and shepherdesses in the Forest of Arden
are apparently well educated, and have no need of the
services of a professional letter-writer. Yet, if we did
not know to the contrary, we should think Phebe
must have employed one. This is the sort of stereo-
typed thing the parish letter-writer *would* turn out :

If the scorn of your bright eyne
Have power to raise such love in mine,
Alack, in me what strange effect
Would they work in mild aspect !
Whiles you chid me, I did love :
How then might your prayers move ?
He that brings this love to thee
Little knows this love in me ;
And by him seal up thy mind ;
Whether that thy youth and kind
Will the faithful offer take
Of me, and all that I can make :
Or else by him my love deny,
And then I'll study how to die.

I don't know whether it was the custom in Shakespeare's time for women of rank to rely on their
stewards to write their letters for them. But in *All's
Well that Ends Well* Bertram's mother instructs her

steward, Rinaldo, to write to her son for her, and
leaves him to compose the letter :

> Write, write, Rinaldo,
> To this unworthy husband of his wife.
> Let every word weigh heavy of her worth
> That he does weigh too light.   My greatest grief,
> Though little he do feel it, set down sharply.

Rinaldo evidently did his job well, for we hear later
on that the letter ' stings Bertram's nature ', and that
on the reading of it ' he changed almost into another
man '.   Bertram ends his letter to his mother with
' My duty to you '.   He is not on good terms with her,
but he does not forget to be externally filial and polite.
An odious young man, yet Helena, whom he treats so
outrageously, is annoyingly infatuated with him.

> Thus, Indian-like,
> Religious in mine error, I adore
> The sun, that looks upon his worshipper,
> But knows of him no more.

My next letter-writer, Leonatus in *Cymbeline*, plays
his wife a dirty trick.   But in all ages a man whose
jealousy is roused is forgiven much.   Leonatus is
devoted to Imogen, yet he can make her chastity the
subject of a wager with a man who scoffs at the idea of
any woman being chaste.

He writes and asks her to welcome this man of

whom he has every reason to think ill. He goes so far as to describe Iachimo to her as ' one of the noblest note, to whose kindnesses I am most infinitely tied. Reflect upon him accordingly, as you value your trust.' ' So far I read aloud ', says Imogen ; and adds that the rest of the letter warms ' the very middle of my heart ',—a letter written by a husband who cannot believe in her fidelity to him without proof, and has sent a comparative stranger to test her virtue !

It is not surprising that when Iachimo returns with his catalogue of all the furniture in Imogen's room, and a careful description of the mole on her left breast, ' cinque-spotted, like the crimson drops i' the bottom of a cowslip ', Leonatus should ' see red ' ; but there is really no excuse for his sitting down and writing a base falsehood to lure his wife to her death. How differently Imogen behaves when Iachimo traduces Leonatus to her ! She is not only indignant ; she is reasonable and sensible. When he urges her to be revenged, she says that, if it were true,—but she will not let her heart be abused in haste by her ears,—revenge would not help her. And what wisdom there is in her reply to Iachimo :

> If thou wert honourable,
> Thou wouldst have told this tale for virtue, not
> For such an end thou seek'st.

She sees through this man, but naturally does not see through this letter from Leonatus :

Justice, and your father's wrath, should he take me in his dominion, could not be so cruel to me, as you, O the dearest of creatures, would even renew me with your eyes.   Take notice that I am in Cambria, at Milford Haven : what your own love will out of this advise you, follow.   So he wishes you all happiness, that remains loyal to his vow, and your, increasing in love,

LEONATUS POSTHUMUS.

There is not a word in this letter to make Imogen doubt its sincerity.   Even a wife, made suspicious by a guilty conscience, could not find anything in it to alarm her.   The trap has been skilfully laid for the unfaithful wife Posthumus believes Imogen to be, and she who is faithful and devoted is an easy prey. She is in such an ecstasy of joy at the thought of the reunion with her lord that it is natural she should not observe the strange demeanour of her lord's servant, Pisanio, who has delivered the letter.   Posthumus has written a second letter to Pisanio, a brutal letter ordering the poor fellow to put Imogen to death.

That I should murder her. . . . *I ! Her !*

Those shameful words,—

'Do't : the letter

That I have sent her, by her own command
Shall give thee opportunity.'—

are pounding in Pisanio's brain, making his heart sick
while Imogen goes into transports of delight over the
journey to 'blessed Milford':

O, for a horse with wings! Hear'st thou, Pisanio?
He is at Milford Haven: read, and tell me
How far 'tis thither. If one of mean affairs
May plod it in a week, why may not I
Glide thither in a day? Then, true Pisanio,
Who long'st, like me, to see thy lord: who long'st—
O, let me bate, but not like me—yet long'st
But in a fainter kind:—O, not like me;
For mine's beyond beyond—say . . . how far it is
To this same blessed Milford, and by the way
Tell me how Wales was made so happy as
To inherit such a haven!

When Imogen reads her husband's letter to Pisanio
it is a horrible shock to her. 'I, false!' She is
appalled at his believing it. *She* had not believed when
he was slandered. His desire to be revenged, to
punish her with death, seems to her a trifle in compari-
son with his want of faith in her. But she is one who
never does things by halves. Love, compelling her to
forgive, she forgives with all her heart. Posthumus,
when he finds he has been deceived, calls himself

' a credulous fool ', and other harsh names, but Imogen refrains from rubbing it in. The nearest thing to a reproach she utters is :

Why did you throw your wedded lady from you ?

Then, without pausing for an answer, she says with extravagant generosity :

Think that you are upon a rock, and now
Throw me again.

To love when all goes well is very easy. To love when the loved one has behaved like Posthumus is not so easy. It requires a self-abnegation which is rare in women, but rarer still in men !

Macbeth's letter to his wife is interesting, not only because it is one of those rare tributes that a man some-times pays to the share his wife has had in the making of his career, but because of the light it throws on the visionary element in Macbeth's character. The goal of his ambition is a material thing,—an earthly crown, —but he believes in the supernatural nature of his ' call '.

They met me in the day of success ; and I have learned by the perfectest report, they have more in them than mortal knowledge. When I burned in desire to question them further, they made themselves air, into which they vanished. Whiles I stood rapt in the wonder of it, came missives from the King, who all-hailed me ' Thane of Cawdor ' ; by which title, before, these weird sisters saluted me, and referred me to the coming on of time, with ' Hail, King that shalt be ! ' This have I thought good to deliver thee, my dearest partner of greatness, that thou mightst not lose the dues of rejoicing, by being ignorant of what greatness is promised thee. Lay it to thy heart, and farewell.

' My dearest partner of greatness ! ' Is not that a wonderful revelation of the relationship between this husband and his wife ? Is not the whole letter a wonderful revelation of the man's character ? A man who was driven by dreams into crime.

As an example of Shakespeare's skill in turning the dramatic device of the letter to other purposes than that of explanation, Bellario's letter to the Duke in *The Merchant of Venice* is about the best one could choose. Besides being a model of what a letter should be, clear, succinct, fine in sound as well as in sense, it is a masterly preparation for Portia's entrance in the Court Scene, and an instruction as to how the actress ought to play that scene. Portia is not to behave with feminine inconsequence and provoke laughter by her ignorance of legal procedure, but to conduct herself like a trained advocate. The letter makes Portia's success in the rôle of a learned young doctor of Rome convincing to the audience.

Your grace shall understand that at the receipt of your letter I am very sick ; but in the instant that your messenger came, in loving visitation was with me a young doctor of Rome. His name is Balthasar. I acquainted him with the cause in controversy between the Jew and Antonio the merchant. We turned o'er many books together. He is furnished with my opinion ; which, bettered with his own learning, the greatness whereof I cannot enough commend, comes with him, at my importunity, to fill up your grace's request in my stead. I beseech you, let his lack of years be no impediment to let him lack a reverend estimation ; for I never knew so young a body with so old a head. I leave him to your gracious acceptance, whose trial shall better publish his commendation.

What a lot of things there are to think over in this letter ! And what pictures it conjures up ! No Italian painter could make us see more clearly the learned Bellario receiving his young visitor and instructing her how to conduct her case. Shakespeare, with the vision of genius, saw Italy when he was writing *The Merchant of Venice* as when he was writing *Julius Caesar* he saw ancient Rome. It may be true, as Ben Jonson reports, that he knew 'small Latin and less Greek ', but that did not hinder his making this letter of warning to Caesar typically Latin in its conciseness :

> Caesar, beware of Brutus ; take heed of Cassius ; come not near Casca ; have an eye to Cinna ; trust not Trebonius ; mark well Metellus Cimber ; Decius Brutus loves thee not ; thou hast wronged Caius Ligarius. There is but one mind in all these men, and it is bent against Caesar. If thou beest not immortal, look about you ; security gives way to conspiracy. The mighty gods defend thee ! Thy lover,
>
> ARTEMIDORUS.

The whole plot of the play and the guiding motive of each character can be found in these pithy sentences.

If we compare this letter with the long-winded effusion from Armado to the King in *Love's Labour's Lost* we get a good idea of the infinite variety of style that the dramatist had at his command, and of his insight into the characteristics of different races at different times. He knew that the Romans were masters of brevity. He knew that the Italianate Elizabethan euphuists were masters of verbosity. And he can reproduce the style of both to the life.

In *Henry IV* Hotspur reads a letter, and this time it is the man who reads it, not the man who writes it, on whom our attention is concentrated. We see a quick-witted, courageous fellow, impatient of cautious people who see both sides of a question and are afraid of going too far. We see the 'extremist', with all his good points and his bad ones. 'But, for mine own part, my lord', writes Hotspur's correspondent, 'I could be well contented to be there, in respect of the love I bear your house '.

Hotspur

He could be contented ; why is he not, then ? In respect of the love he bears our house ; he shows in this, he loves his own barn better than he loves our house. . . . [*reads*] 'The purpose you undertake is dangerous.' Why, that's certain ! 'Tis dangerous to take a cold, to sleep, to drink; but I tell you, my lord fool, out of this nettle, danger, we pluck this flower, safety. ' The purpose you undertake is dangerous ; the friends you have named uncertain ; the time itself unsorted, and your whole plot too light for the counterpoise of so great an opposition.' Say you so, say you so ? I say unto you again : you are a shallow, cowardly hind, and you lie. What a lack-brain is this ! By the Lord, our plot is a good plot as ever was laid ; our friends true and constant : a good plot, good friends, and full of expectation ; an excellent plot, very good friends ! What a frosty-spirited rogue is this ! Why, my lord of York commends the plot and the general course of the action. 'Zounds, an I were now by this rascal, I could brain him with his lady's fan.

There is real 'vinegar and pepper' in this outburst of Hotspur's. Compare it with the mock 'vinegar and pepper' of Sir Andrew Aguecheek's swaggering challenge to Viola in *Twelfth Night*. Sir Andrew is, as you know, a very devil of a fellow. He is quite sure that this letter is bold enough to strike terror into the heart of the most confident enemy :

Youth, whatsoever thou art, thou art but a scurvy fellow. Wonder not, nor admire not in thy mind, why I do call thee so, for I will show thee no reason for't. Thou comest to the lady Olivia, and in my sight she uses thee kindly ; but thou liest in thy throat ; that is not the matter I challenge thee for. I will waylay thee going home ; where if it be thy chance to kill me, thou killest me like a rogue and a villain. Fare thee well, and God have mercy upon one of our souls ! He may have mercy upon mine ; but my hope is better, and so look to thyself.

Thy friend, as thou usest him, and thy sworn enemy,   ANDREW AGUECHEEK.

Besides Hamlet's letter to Ophelia, there are two other letters from him in the play which are often omitted in acting versions. The first is to Horatio, and manifests Hamlet's complete confidence in his one loyal friend :

Horatio, when thou shalt have overlooked this, give these fellows some means to the King ; they have letters for him. Ere we were two days old at sea, a pirate of very warlike appointment gave us chase. Finding ourselves too slow of sail, we put on a compelled valour, and in the grapple I boarded them. On the instant they got clear of our ship, so I alone became their prisoner. They have dealt with me like thieves of mercy, but they knew what they did : I am to do a good turn for them. Let the King have the letters I have sent, and repair thou to me with as much speed as thou wouldst fly death. I have words to speak in thine ear will make thee dumb, yet are they much too light for the bore of the matter. These good fellows will bring thee where I am. Rosencrantz and Guildenstern hold their course for England ; of them I have much to tell thee. Farewell.

He that thou knowest thine,   HAMLET.

The actual words of the second letter, to the King, are harmless enough, yet somehow they convey a threat. ' What is he driving at ? ' Claudius is puzzled ; he can make nothing of these studiously civil lines, and reads them to Laertes to find out what impression they make on him :

High and mighty, You shall know I am set naked on your kingdom. To-morrow shall I beg leave to see your kingly eyes ; when I shall, first asking your pardon thereunto, recount the occasion of my sudden and more strange return.   HAMLET.

'Naked !' Claudius exclaims. 'And in a post-script here he adds "alone".'

In *Antony and Cleopatra*, Shakespeare adopts the method of making someone give the substance of a letter, instead of reading the actual words of the writer. Twice Octavius Caesar enters 'reading a letter', and twice we have to trust to his honour that he is giving a fair summary of the contents. His account of the letter which brings news of Antony is probably coloured by his jealousy of the great rival. I feel he is exaggerating when he says :

> From Alexandria
> This is the news : he fishes, drinks, and wastes
> The lamps of night in revel ; is not more manlike
> Than Cleopatra ; nor the Queen of Ptolemy
> More womanly than he ; hardly gave audience, or
> Vouchsafed to think he had partners. You shall find there
> A man who is the abstract of all faults
> That all men follow.

Octavius is anxious to justify himself in the eyes of the world for hating Antony, and what more likely than that he should make the most of anything his correspondent has written to Antony's discredit ?

Antony was, as he is represented here, a voluptuary, a hard drinker and a great guzzler. But he was also a great soldier, and a great leader of men. He loved luxury, yet he set an example to his subordinates in bearing the hardships and privations of war with fortitude. It is said he refused all comforts denied to the rank and file. It was only when he was ' on leave ' that his cooks had to put a fresh boar on the spit every hour so that he could dine when he pleased. So that ' abstract of all faults that all men follow ' is a misrepresentation. Shakespeare emphasises one of his faults, a tendency to ' talk big ' and strike big attitudes. His challenge to take Octavius on in single combat is an example of this weakness.

Octavius exclaims : ' He calls me boy ' (this time Octavius's words ring true, and we feel he is reporting the incident accurately) :

> And chides as he had power
> To beat me out of Egypt.   My messenger
> He hath whipped with rods ; dares me to personal
>   combat !
> Caesar to Antony ! Let the old ruffian know
> I have many other ways to die.

Timon of Athens's last message to the world is melancholy reading ! Our ' gentle Shakespeare ' can be fiercely and savagely cynical at times. Timon makes his grave on the ' beached verge of the salt flood ', and erects his own tomb ' upon the very hem o' the sea '.

A soldier takes an impression in wax of the inscription scratched on it, and brings it to Alcibiades :

Here lies a wretched corse, of wretched soul bereft.
Seek not my name : a plague consume you wicked
    caitiffs left !
Here lie I, Timon, who, alive, all living men did hate.
Pass by and curse thy fill, but pass and stay not
    here thy gait.

Alcibiades, with a generosity that we should imitate, finds the noble element in this last effort at consistency of a consistent hater of men :

These well express in thee thy latter spirits :
Though thou abhorr'dst in us our human griefs,
Scorn'dst our brain's flow and those our droplets
    which
From niggard nature fall, yet rich conceit
Taught thee to make vast Neptune weep for aye
On thy low grave, on faults forgiven.

Those are appropriate words with which to bring this little study of an unfrequented corner of the great world of Shakespeare's mind to an end ! ' My faults forgiven ' I know, I say farewell.

PRINTED IN GREAT BRITAIN BY ROBERT MACLEHOSE AND CO. LTD.
THE UNIVERSITY PRESS, GLASGOW